"I Do" *or* Do I?

J. Robin Maxson
with Garry Friesen

HARVEST HOUSE PUBLISHERS
EUGENE, OREGON

Cover design by Dugan Design Group, Bloomington, Minnesota

Cover photo © Rubberball / Alamy

Backcover photo by sjharmon.com

The author is represented by MacGregor Literary, Inc.

This book contains stories in which the author has changed people's names and some details of their situations in order to protect their privacy.

"I DO" OR DO I?
Copyright © 2014 by James Robin Maxson
Published by Harvest House Publishers
Eugene, Oregon 97402
www.harvesthousepublishers.com

Library of Congress Cataloging-in-Publication Data
Maxson, J. Robin, 1947-
I do or do I? / J. Robin Maxson, with Garry Friesen.
pages cm
ISBN 978-0-7369-4547-9 (pbk.)
ISBN 978-0-7369-4548-6 (eBook)
1. Marriage—Religious aspects—Christianity. 2. Mate selection—Religious aspects—Christianity. 3. Decision making—Religious aspects—Christianity. I. Title.
BV835.M287 2014
248.4—dc23

2013031649

Printed in the United States of America

14 15 16 17 18 19 20 21 22 / VP-JH / 10 9 8 7 6 5 4 3 2 1

To my children,
Rachel Maxson
and
Michael Evans-Maxson,
who inspired this book,
and whose pursuit of godly living
put its principles on display.

You show that you are a letter from Christ delivered by us,
written not with ink but with the Spirit of the living God,
not on tablets of stone but on tablets of human hearts.
(2 Corinthians 3:3 ESV)

Contents

INTRODUCTION

"You know what I wish?"

The young woman, midthirties, sitting opposite me in my office, was wiping tears from her eyes. We had spent the previous forty-five minutes processing the demise of her seven-year marriage to Eric. Sherry was a lifelong Christian—a preacher's kid. Eric had come to faith through her father's ministry two years before their wedding. Fundamental differences in personality, background, worldview, goals and priorities, and marital expectations eroded and ultimately overwhelmed a promising beginning. Eric's affair extinguished Sherry's hope for a miracle that never materialized.

"You know what I wish?"

In the momentary pause between Sherry's question and her answer, several possible scenarios flashed through my mind. Having spent the last three months laboring with this couple—praying, instructing, negotiating, pleading, weeping—doing everything possible to rescue and restore their marriage, I knew what I wished. My list was long. But it didn't include the one thing on Sherry's mind.

"My parents knew that my decision to marry Eric was a mistake. *I wish they had said something.*"

Something Needs to Be Said

Countless individuals, reviewing with hindsight a decision-making process that led to disaster, wish the same thing. (Maybe you're one of them.) We know better, of course. We know we can't hit rewind and get a do-over on our mistakes. We also know that no amount of insight from whatever source can *guarantee* an ideal outcome. But those who, like Sherry, pay the price for faulty choices often come to recognize they would have been better served by some helpful guidance from objective and wise advisors.

"I wish they had said something."

We can't turn back the clock for Sherry and Eric, or anyone else. But we can be proactive in an effort to prevent recurrences of their scenario. While we can't address the specifics of any particular situation, we can say something that may well head off commonly made mistakes while offering constructive guidance that brings wisdom to bear on the choices singles make.

In this book, then, we will consider two categories of information that target two legitimate goals in marital decision making. One objective is *negative*—the desire to avoid catastrophic consequences. So we will attempt to expose and correct erroneous ways of thinking that could lead to detrimental decisions. The other goal is decidedly *positive*—to make choices that have the best chance of producing beneficial marital outcomes, whether one remains single or gets married.

Considering the Source

Sound good?

Maybe. When something needs to be said, it matters a great deal who is doing the talking. If you are turning to someone for counsel, that input is valuable only if the ideas shared are actually insightful. A lot of people have opinions, but they can't all be right. The issues in question really matter. So it is very important to consider the source.

Is this book a reliable source of guidance for marital decision making?

I kind of feel like I'm applying for a job. You're less than a dozen paragraphs into this book, so you don't have to hire me; you can bail out without having lost much time. You probably don't know much about me, so why should you read this book?

The best I can do is tell you a little about where I'm coming from and give a sneak preview of some of the ideas we'll explore in these pages.

Cultural Chaos

I'll begin with an observation. In the decade that I've devoted to studying singleness and marriage, I've become convinced of a stunning reality: *The venture of marital decision making is more complex today than it ever has been.*

Ever.

I'm not kidding.

The main reason for this daunting state of affairs is the cultural environment in which singles carry out their decision making. Societal perspectives on marriage, singleness, dating, and sex have undergone tremendous changes in an incredibly brief span of time. How dramatic have these changes been? Writing in 2005, historian Stephanie Coontz summarized: "The current rearrangement of both married and single life is in fact without historical precedent."[1] And in another place she says, "The role of marriage in society and personal life has changed more in the past 30 years than in the previous 3,000."[2]

Let me translate: If you are thirty-five years old or younger, the ways that members of your generation think about marriage and singleness are strikingly different from the perspectives of virtually all human beings who have preceded you on this planet. That fact, all by itself, does not determine which point of view is right, or even better. You just need to know that the cultural factors that influence marital decision making are very different than they used to be.

We will examine the nature of those changes in the pages to follow. But if you have found it difficult to sort out your thinking about marriage, or have found that moving in that direction is complicated, you are not imagining things. I don't know if acquiring a mate has ever been easy, but marital decision making has never been more complicated than it is today.

As messy as things have become, it is not difficult to understand either the problem or the solution. The fundamental problem is that humanity has deviated from God's design for both marriage and singleness. Now there is a law of nature that applies to everything in the universe—including human beings: *If you violate the design, sooner or later bad things will happen.* When God made human beings in his image, he also established guidelines for healthy relationships. Recent efforts to improve on the original design are actually counterproductive. We are not smarter than our Creator. And bad things are happening.

If I am right about the problem, I think anyone can see the solution. Dr. Joe Aldrich, past president of Multnomah Bible College, used to say, "Get on the right side of how things work." That is good advice. We need to get back in harmony with the divine design. But if the solution is simple to describe, it is not easy to achieve. For starters, you have to examine God's blueprints, and that will take some effort. But it is doable, and I hope you will take it on.

Divine Wisdom

I believe the Bible is true and view it as an owner's manual for human beings. I share the apostle Peter's confidence that God's "divine power has bestowed on us everything necessary for life and godliness" (2 Peter 1:3). In my experience, it has served as a reliable guide to life.

I look to the Bible, then, to correct mistaken ideas (2 Timothy 3:16). When I declare my intention to expose and correct erroneous ways of thinking that could lead to detrimental decisions, my primary point of reference is the teaching of Holy Scripture. So while I have made an effort to research the contributions of other fields of knowledge (such as history and the social sciences) to our understanding of human relationships, I have put more effort into constructing an accurate picture of biblical teaching. My understanding of that instruction is the standard by which all human input is evaluated.

On the other hand, the Scriptures provide guidance for right thinking and acting (Proverbs 3:5-7). Our Creator-Redeemer continues to supply all the resources we need to make wise decisions about singleness and marriage. Indeed, I devote the greater percentage of this book's content to identifying the principles and provisions available for our guidance and implementation.

I do not intend to defend my convictions here.[3] Nor do I assume that every reader will share them. But I think it is important for you to know what I consider to be the basis of the authority with which I approach these subjects. The only reason I can presume to address the complex issues of marital decision making is that Someone Else already has. I do not claim originality; I am basically reporting news—some bad, some good, all of it beneficial.

If you share my convictions about the reliability of the Bible, I hope you will be encouraged that this book is attempting to shed scriptural light on the chaos of our time. If you are uncertain or skeptical about the relevance of biblical guidance for contemporary issues, I invite you to at least consider this approach. I believe that truth is self-authenticating—that is, it will demonstrate its truthfulness to those who are open to recognize it. Maybe this presentation will open the door to a more hopeful path to follow.

Modern Myths

Now, having expressed great confidence in the reliability of the Bible, I need to add the caveat that readers can misinterpret its meaning. And I believe that has happened. For example, many Christians have been taught that they can expect God to tell them whether to marry and whom they should marry. While I respect those who hold this view, I think they have misread the scriptural passages related to this subject. And if I am right about that, it is important to correct that misunderstanding.

Other discrepancies need to be addressed as well—commonly held beliefs where conventional wisdom diverges from divine wisdom. In the following chapters, we will consider five common myths that need to be exposed and corrected.[4] As with all myths that are widely accepted, each one contains a measure of truth, which lends to its credibility. But judged from a biblical perspective, there is something wrong and hazardous with each of them.

- *Myth 1*: A Christian can expect God to tell him or her whether and whom to marry.
- *Myth 2*: Singleness should be thought of as a transitional stage of life that is preparatory for the "completion" of marriage.

- *Myth 3*: The key to a successful marriage is to find and marry one's soul mate.
- *Myth 4*: The best way to determine compatibility with a prospective mate is to live together.
- *Myth 5*: The most important criterion for a good marital match is chemistry.

If, as you read through the list of myths, you found yourself asking, "I wonder what's wrong with that one?" you probably need to read this book.

My Hope for You

One last thing about my perspective: I am completely neutral as to whether *you* should get married. I do not believe that everyone who is single will or even should get married. My writing partner, Garry Friesen, is a lifelong bachelor who has lived a full, rich life. He could still marry (he ain't dead yet), but he doesn't think he has to in order to be a complete human being. He has seized the advantages of his single state to advance the kingdom of God and has experienced great fulfillment in that stewardship.

On the other hand, I believe that most single adults are prewired for marriage. We were created with a built-in predisposition to seek out a mate and establish a new family. So single people think about getting married, intend to get married, and most actually do so. I assume that most readers are inclined in that direction and are looking for guidance to that end.

My hope for you personally is *not* that you will remain single or get married. My hope is that whichever course you take, you will make wise decisions. I hope you will know the goodness of God in every circumstance of life. I hope you will find fulfillment and contentment in whatever marital state you find yourself and that you will experience the sufficiency of Christ and the abundance of his grace for godly living. At every stage of your life, I hope you will know the joy of contributing to God's kingdom and exalting his glory. That's what I'm praying for as I write.

Deciding What Should Be Said

When I began this project almost ten years ago, I wasn't responding specifically to the problems of Sherry and Eric. My own children, Rachel and Mike, having reached their midtwenties, challenged me to address an issue they had encountered. As they began to engage in marital decision making, they were struck by how befuddled so many of their peers seemed to be. Misinformation and confusion were rampant. They realized that some resource was needed that could guide Christian single adults to make wise choices that are biblically informed.

They thought I could help because I had previously assisted Garry Friesen in writing *Decision Making and the Will of God.*[5] In this landmark work, Dr. Friesen challenged the prevailing model of divine guidance and proposed an alternative—the Way of Wisdom—that better explained and applied biblical revelation. Rachel's vision was that I would write a book that would apply the principles of the Way of Wisdom to marital decision making.

As I began my research, I could find nothing that brought together an explanation of God's design for decision making, marriage, singleness, and sexuality. *How can individuals make choices that are in harmony with God's design if they don't know what that design is?*, I wondered. So I set out to write a book that would summarize the biblical instruction on those topics and then apply the principles to the process of looking for a mate.

That project was the centerpiece of my doctor of ministry research project (Dallas Theological Seminary, 2009). It culminated in 2012 in the publication of *Singleness, Marriage, and the Will of God: A Comprehensive Biblical Guide* (Harvest House Publishers).

"I Do" or Do I? is intended to be a reader-friendly adaptation of that more academic text. This volume is shorter and less technical,[6] and because I keep learning, some new material appears in this book that was not in its predecessor.[7] We hope this edition will make the content more accessible to more readers.

I am telling you all this so that you will know I've tried to be diligent in doing my homework. This book is not simply a collection of sermons strung together in printed form. It is a serious attempt to provide biblical instruction to those considering serious decisions. Based on what other readers have reported, I expect that you will learn things from this book that you didn't know before—ideas and insights that are truly useful. I know I was surprised by how much I learned in writing the book.

In both of these editions I have benefitted from the assistance of Garry Friesen, my colleague and writing partner. Besides authoring *Decision Making and the Will of God,* Dr. Friesen was professor of Bible and theology at Multnomah University for thirty-seven years. While at Multnomah, Dr. G opened his home to provide housing for male students. Over a period of twelve years, he mentored over eighty young men living in community at "Aslan's How." He also served as chairman of the council of elders for Imago Dei Community, a vibrant church whose ministry reaches beyond the Portland area to the world. What I hope you can recognize is that Garry has not only a wealth of biblical knowledge but also extensive experience in providing spiritual guidance to young single adults. And, having never married, Dr. G offers the indispensable perspective of a lifelong single man. While I am the lead author of this book, Garry has been looking over my shoulder throughout.

Something Needs to Be Read

In this book, you will read about five things. Actually, you will read about five *different* things—several times. To be specific, you will encounter

- five myths to be debunked
- five ingredients in the recipe for compatibility
- five stages of courtship
- five tasks of a plan for looking for a mate
- the "top ten" missteps to a miserable marriage (that's five doubled)

But the most important quintet was the set I discovered after I had written about all the others.

5 Keys to Wise Marital Decision Making

When I completed *Singleness, Marriage, and the Will of God,* I read back through what I had written and asked, "Can I boil all this material down to the essential keys to making wise marital decisions?" It turns out there are five of them, and in that book, we put them at the end because that's where I figured them out.

But in this book, I'm going to list them right up front so you can get an idea of what we're going to be talking about in the following chapters.

To make sound choices, you will need to

1. Understand and commit to God's design (for decision making, singleness, sexuality, and marriage).
2. Pray *for* wisdom and *about* your desires.
3. Grow up and become a healthy, maturing adult.
4. Make relational choices that are moral and wise.
5. Prepare well together if you find a suitable prospect for marriage.

These five keys are equal in importance, but they are not equal in size. That is to say, Key 1 gets the lion's share of attention in this book—that's what parts 1, 2, and 3 are about. On the other hand, I say very little about Key 5. It is critical to wise decision making, but it is beyond the scope of this volume. The other keys are distributed here and there throughout the text.

To utilize these keys, you need to comprehend what they mean. To do that, you need to read the rest of the book. And I hope you won't read it by yourself. The value of working through this material will be greatly increased if you do it with a friend—or better yet, a small group of friends. Make good use of the "Questions for Reflection and Group Discussion" available from the website: www.TheMarriageDecision

.com. Open a journal on your computer where you can record the thoughts, questions, and ideas provoked by your interaction with this material.

And know that I am praying with you as you engage Key 2 (James 1:5).

Going Further—Webpage

In an effort to make *"I Do" or Do I?* accessible to more readers, I have restricted the content of this book to the information that is most essential. Additional material that may be of interest to some readers is available online at www.TheMarriageDecision.com. At that site, you can find

- the endnotes: Scripture references, complete source information for quotations, and supplementary content
- Questions for Reflection and Group Discussion: to help readers explore the implications of each chapter on their own or with a group
- Frequently Asked Questions and other articles related to the subject of marital decision making

Part 1

God's Design for Decision Making

Modern Myth 1

As a Christian, you can expect God to tell you whether to marry and whom to marry.

INTRODUCTION TO PART 1

God's Design for Decision Making

Tom and Sandee grew up in different parts of the country. When they met as freshmen at a Christian college, the romantic sparks flew and they fell in love. Less than two months after they met, they announced their engagement to be married.

I know about this couple and their experience because my daughter, Rachel, was a dorm mate to Sandee. Alarmed by their announcement, Rachel wrote to me: "Sandee talks about how she feels 'convicted' to marry Tom, and she just knows this is God's will, because she feels totally at peace about it. Just about everyone on this floor thinks she's making a huge mistake, but when she walks up we smile and say, 'Congratulations.'"

Tom and Sandee's friends had good reason for concern. Later in this book, I describe the "Top Ten Missteps to a Miserable Marriage" (chapter 10). It's a tongue-in-cheek guide to foolish decision making. But Tom and Sandee were acting as if they had read that list and had decided to follow it! Of the ten missteps described, they were implementing *at least* six of them. But while their classmates could recognize twitterpation when they saw it, there was little those classmates could say. Not only Tom and Sandee but everyone around them had bought in to Myth 1 of marital decision making: "As a Christian, you can expect God to tell you whether and whom to marry." If God told them to do it, who could say that their decision to marry was foolish?

But did God tell them to get married? I strongly doubt it. Rather, following a system of guidance taught by well-meaning Christian leaders, Tom and Sandee apparently *interpreted* a combination of outward conditions and inward impressions as the leading of the Lord. It is not uncommon for enraptured individuals to mistake the influence of hormones for the voice of the Holy Spirit—especially when those feelings are reinforced by favorable circumstances. The supporting theology of guidance provides no check on the judgment-impairing influence of romantic passion, but rather tends to shut off outside sources of wisdom that could be really helpful.[1]

If I had been given the opportunity to express my concerns to Tom and Sandee, they might justifiably have responded, "If God doesn't tell us what choices to make, on what basis are we to make right decisions?" The alternative would seem to be that we are left to our own devices—to do the best we can on our own and hope it turns out well.

Reducing our decision-making options to these two either-or possibilities is an exercise in simplistic thinking. Tom and Sandee were employing childish reasoning to make grown-up decisions. What they (and their friends) needed was an adult understanding of God's design for decision making.

To get to that understanding, we must consider a very basic question: Is there such a thing as Christian decision making? Do believers in Christ approach their choices differently or the same as everyone else?

Christian Decision Making?

"So how's that working for you?"

For years, that single diagnostic question by psychologist Phil McGraw has exposed the flaws in dysfunctional patterns of thinking of guests on the *Dr. Phil* show. Defective decision making eventually produces detrimental outcomes. And Dr. Phil is quite skillful at connecting the dots between cause and effect.

But that question does more than uncover faulty reasoning. It also reveals the criterion by which our decisions are judged. For we all hope to make choices that will bring about beneficial results—for us. Indeed, as we shall see later on this book, the dominant motivation for most people in marital decision making is, what will make *me* happy? What will meet *my* needs? When social scientists attempt to measure whether certain choices produce outcomes that are favorable or unfavorable, their standard of measurement is "marital satisfaction." In other words, how's that working for you?

Do Christians approach decision making differently? The answer is yes. Believers have motivations, priorities, and goals that are poles apart from non-Christians. These differences stem from a transformed *identity* brought about by a change of *relationship*.

I can best explain this by a couple of analogies.

Tomorrow, I plan to eat supper at a Chinese restaurant. If I were still a bachelor, that wouldn't be happening. I don't hate Asian food, but it is not my favorite cuisine. But now I am married, and Louise enjoys sweet-and-sour dishes—and tomorrow is her birthday. So we are eating at Wong's because I love my wife. My desire to please her vastly outweighs my gastronomic preferences. My decision making is governed by my identity as a loving husband who is in relationship (delightedly so) with a wonderful wife.

Second analogy. Louise is the manager of Basin Book Trader, a used bookstore. One aspect of her job is to purchase used books for resale by the store. She obtains books from customers and also scours thrift stores and garage sales for promising stock. Her goal: profit for the store. To that end, she spends the owner's money to acquire books that she hopes will sell. She is not looking for books *she* would enjoy reading; she is looking for books she believes *other people* would want to read. She is not shopping as a consumer; she is shopping as a manager. Her decision making is governed by her identity as a book buyer whose relationship to the owner is that of an employee. The benefit to her is indirect—if she succeeds, the owner prospers and Louise remains gainfully employed.

Do you see the principle? *Decision making is governed by identity, which is determined by relationship*. In the first instance, I want to please my wife because, as her husband, I love her. In the second instance, Louise seeks to promote the profitability of the store (and please the owner) because she is a dedicated employee. In neither case are we acting independently, pursuing our own interests. Because of who we have *become* (a husband and a manager), we make choices aimed at advancing the cause of another.

We can see similar perspectives in the spiritual realm. On two different occasions, and in two different ways, Jesus answered the question, "What is the most important thing?"

> "You must love the Lord your God with all your heart, all your soul, and all your mind. This is the *first* and *greatest* commandment" (Matthew 22:37-38 NLT).

> "*Above all* pursue [God's] kingdom and righteousness, and all these things will be given to you as well" (Matthew 6:33).

As a Christian, my greatest *affection* is to be for the Lord who is my heavenly Father (Matthew 6:32). My greatest *ambition* is to be for the advancement of his rule and his righteousness in my own life (spiritual growth) and in my world (mission). I am not the King. He is. I am a child of the King. And so, in my life, my affection and my ambition are unified. For *the One I work for is the One I love.*

Here, then, is the core difference between autonomous decision making and Christian decision making: "We make it our ambition to please [the Lord]" (2 Corinthians 5:9).

- My motivation: love for my heavenly Father.
- My priority: the advancement of his rule and righteousness.
- My goal: to please him.

Now this does not mean that Christians have no other ambitions or affections. Nor does it mean that every decision I make will directly and observably advance God's rule.[2] Sometimes you just need to choose which box of cereal you're going to open for breakfast. It does mean that Christians have a hierarchy of values—some things are more important than others. "*Above all* pursue his kingdom and righteousness." If I do that, "all these (other) things" will fall into their proper (secondary) place.

This is a book about marital decision making—those choices that perpetuate singleness or lead to marriage. If you are hoping to make wise decisions, the first step is to have a firm grasp on *who you are* as a decision maker. If you think this is all about you, or even mainly about you (and your spouse), you will stumble out of the gate. If you are acting as the king or queen of your realm with the goal of enhancing your own kingdom, you are short-sighted and will be disappointed. But if you make marital decisions from the standpoint of being a child of the King and a manager of his resources for the sake of his kingdom, both your priorities and your thinking will be rightly ordered. And the personal benefits of your marital decision making will more likely be enjoyed as a by-product of your commitment to Christ.

Pleasing God

Now I know what will please Louise (Chinese food); and she knows how to please her boss (sell lots of books). But how does a Christian know what is pleasing to God?

A very good answer is provided by the apostle Paul: "we have not ceased praying for you and asking God to fill you with *the knowledge of his will* in all spiritual wisdom and understanding, so that you may live worthily of the Lord and *please him in all respects*" (Colossians 1:9-10).

This passage answers our question about how to please God, and it starts with the knowledge of and obedience to his will. The source of this knowledge is God himself who imparts it as a resource for godly living.

This is what Tom and Sandee were claiming that God had done for them. They were simply following his will. But I have reason to believe that while this couple and the apostle Paul were both talking about "God's will," they did not mean the same thing. If I'm right, it is critical for us to understand the apostle's perspective.

That is the subject of the next two chapters.

Don't Forget...

- To make grown-up decisions, we need an adult understanding of God's design for decision making.
- Christian decision making is distinctive in that, as children

of the King and managers of his resources, "we make it our ambition to please [the Lord]" (2 Corinthians 5:8).

To access the endnotes go to:
www.TheMarriageDecision.com

Chapter 1

What's God's Will Got to Do with It?

If I could turn back the clock, I would prefer to engage with Tom and Sandee during their senior year of high school—before cupid struck. And I would offer them a crash course in "Decision Making and the Will of God."[1] Specifically, I would walk them through the biblical principles of guidance that we call the Way of Wisdom. And then I would show them how those principles are consistently applied by Jesus and the apostle Paul to marital decision making.

The Bible's instruction on guidance distinguishes between two kinds of decisions: those that are directly addressed by the Bible and those that are not. For instance, the modern reader will look in vain for any verse commanding her to get married (or to remain single). On the other hand, the Bible has a lot to say about how single persons should behave and how husbands and wives should treat each other. So the Bible provides guidance for some features of singleness and marriage, but there are also many specific decisions Scripture does not directly address. So we must distinguish between the categories of "commanded decisions" and "non-commanded decisions."

As far as the Bible is concerned, Tom and Sandee's determination to marry falls in the second category: non-commanded decisions. That is to say, there is no biblical passage instructing them to get married.

But when biblical writers talk about God's will, they are most often describing the first category: decisions explicitly instructed. When Paul wrote of the importance of being filled with "the knowledge of his will in all spiritual wisdom and understanding," he was referring to

God's *moral* will:[2] all the instructions, commands, and principles God revealed in the Bible that teach us what to believe and how to live.[3]

We will return to Tom and Sandee's decision momentarily. But first we need to identify and affirm the first principle of decision making: *Where God commands, we must obey.*

The Nature of God's Moral Will

In stating this principle so succinctly, I don't want to convey a simplistic impression. The moral will of God is not just a divine to-do list like, say, the Ten Commandments. Nor should we react to the verb *command* as though God were simply giving orders to his underlings.[4] A more complete picture of God's moral will includes four characteristics.

God's Moral Will
At-a-Glance

Its *source*: the moral will of God is *the expression of the character of God* (Psalm 19:7-11; Luke 6:35-36; Romans 7:12).

Its *location*: the moral will of God is *fully revealed in the Bible* (2 Timothy 3:16-17; Hebrews 1:1-2).

Its *scope*: God's moral will *touches every aspect and moment of life* encompassing the believer's goals[5] and attitudes[6]—as well as his actions.[7]

Its *impact*: the moral will of God is able to *equip believers for every good work*, pointing the way to *fullness of life* (Psalm 19:7-11; 2 Timothy 3:16-17).

SUMMARY: Because God is good, his moral will is *good for us* (Joshua 1:8; Deuteronomy 10:12-13; Psalm 1:1-6; John 13:17). "The rules of the LORD are true, and righteous altogether...in keeping them there is great reward" (Psalm 19:9,11 ESV).

Because God's moral will touches every aspect and moment of life and leads to fullness of life, it follows that *the believer's understanding of and proper response to the moral will of God is one of the most important components of decision making that is truly Christian.* The converse is also true: one major reason why people (even Christians) make poor decisions is that they elevate their own reasoning and desires over God's revealed will (Proverbs 3:5-7). When it comes to responding to the moral will of God, the right thing is also the smart thing.

The Way of Wisdom

1. Where God commands, we must obey.

Freedom Within Limits

Now we come to the crux of God's design for decision making. For while the moral will of God provides the framework for every choice we make, it does not directly address every detail of life. It would be impossible for a book written in antiquity to address the options that confront believers in the twenty-first century. So the question emerges, how are believers to make decisions that honor God when he does not tell us specifically what to do in those situations?

Tom and Sandee (and Robin and Garry) were taught that God *will* tell us what to do if we listen for his leading. Teachers of the "ideal will" view of guidance do not usually mean that God will speak to us in an audible voice the way he spoke to Moses from the burning bush. God's guidance today, they say, is imparted through "inner impressions" that represent the "still small voice" of the Spirit. Choices that are "non-commanded" by way of a biblical imperative become "commanded" as the voice of God speaks to the believer's heart. Such inner impressions are supported and confirmed by other "signs," such as circumstances, passages from the Bible, the counsel of other Christians, personal desires, and even common sense. This theology of guidance is the origin for modern myth 1: *As a Christian, you can expect God to tell you whether and whom to marry.*

Without intending any disrespect for fellow Christians who hold this view, I do not find this explanation taught in the Bible.[8] In fact, in those passages that offer the most explicit counsel on marital decision making, at the very point where one might expect a biblical writer to instruct his readers to "seek God's will" for the decision in question, the author takes a different approach.

This different approach was established by God with the very first human being at the beginning of history. In the Creator's instructions to Adam regarding life in the Garden of Eden, he established the principle of freedom within revealed limits.

> Then the LORD God commanded the man, "You may freely eat fruit from every tree of the orchard, but you must not eat from the tree of the knowledge of good and evil, for when you eat from it you will surely die" (Genesis 2:16-17).

In a demonstration of God's goodness, the Creator began this command with a declaration of the extent of Adam's freedom of choice: "You may *freely* eat fruit from *every* tree of the orchard." Then he added the single restriction ("the tree of the knowledge of good and evil") with a clear explanation of the consequence for violation ("you will surely die").

This early direction by God set the pattern for the revelation of his moral will in the centuries that followed. And so the second principle in God's design for decision making may be summarized: *Where there is no command, God gives us the freedom (and responsibility) to choose.*[9]

When we speak of freedom within the moral will of God, our terminology suggests a diagram. God's moral will can be represented by a circle. Whatever is commanded by God lies within the circle; whatever is forbidden by God is outside the circle. Within the larger circle of God's moral will is a smaller circle signifying an area of freedom.

BIBLICAL VIEW OF FREEDOM WITHIN GOD'S MORAL WILL

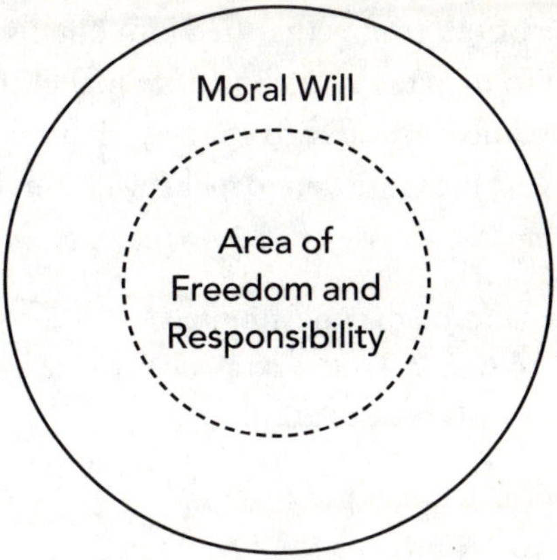

Now in the command given to Adam, the tree of knowledge of good and evil would be outside the circle of God's will—forbidden. The rest of the trees of Eden would not only be inside the larger circle, they would be within the area of freedom.

This second principle has three important ramifications. First, in non-commanded decisions, the Christian's freedom to make a choice is real—God should not be expected to dictate (micromanage) what she must do. Second, when such a decision is made, it must not violate God's moral will in purpose, attitude, or execution. And third, some decisions have multiple options, several of which may be acceptable to God.

THE WAY OF WISDOM

1. Where God commands, we must obey.
2. Where there is no command, God gives us freedom and responsibility to choose.

Criterion for God-Approved Choices

The other side of the coin is that freedom entails responsibility. If God is not going to dictate every choice we make, the believer is not only free to choose, he is *required* to choose. That raises a critical question: On what basis is the Christian to make decisions in freedom areas? Short answer: *wisdom.*

> Plans succeed through good counsel;
> don't go to war without wise advice.
> (Proverbs 20:18 NLT)

> Using a dull ax requires great strength,
> so sharpen the blade.
> That's the value of wisdom;
> it helps you succeed.
> (Ecclesiastes 10:10 NLT)

> Therefore be very careful how you live—not as unwise but as wise, taking advantage of every opportunity, because the days are evil (Ephesians 5:15-16).

Wisdom has been the standard for effective decision making from Day One. We can easily miss this fact when we read our Bibles because the focus of the story line is on God's distinctive (and sometimes unusual) directives to the key players. But when we observe those same people making decisions that have not been dictated by God (non-commanded decisions), they are seeking to apply wisdom. For "wisdom is the power to see, and the inclination to choose, the best and highest goal, together with the surest means of attaining it."[10]

The application of wisdom to decision making permeates the Old Testament. In fact, Bible scholars have designated one major segment of the Hebrew scriptures—Job, Psalms, Proverbs, Ecclesiastes, and Song of Songs—as Wisdom Literature. These writings underscore the value of wisdom for everyday living and decision making.

Jesus built on this tradition in his teaching. He challenged his disciples to be "wise as serpents" (Matthew 10:16). And many of his parables advocated the application of wisdom to the challenges of life (Matthew 7:24-27; Luke 14:25-32).

Especially instructive is the practice of the apostles and the instructions they gave to the churches. When the apostles gave explanations for their non-commanded decisions, here is the terminology they used: "we thought it best" (1 Thessalonians 3:1-2 NIV); "I have considered it necessary" (Philippians 2:25-26); "if it seems advisable" (1 Corinthians 16:3-4); "it is not right" (Acts 6:2-4); "I have decided" (Titus 3:12). When they gave directions in decision making, the apostles' exhortations were consistent with their practice (1 Corinthians 6:1-6; Ephesians 5:15-16; Colossians 4:5).

While the apostles pray for wisdom and instruct us to pray for wisdom (Colossians 1:9; James 1:5), not once do they tell believers to "ask God to tell you what to do" in a given non-commanded decision.

So the Christian's objective in a non-commanded decision is not so much to make the right choice as it is to make a good choice—that is, a wise one. Such a decision is one that has the best chance of accomplishing a legitimate goal without violating the moral will of God. Decisions that are both moral and wise are also pleasing to God.

Acquiring Wisdom

So where does one find this wisdom for decision making? Ultimately, this spiritual wisdom comes from God: "For the LORD gives wisdom, and from his mouth comes knowledge and understanding" (Proverbs 2:6; see also Romans 11:33; 16:27). But this wisdom is not imparted to those who are passive. It is instilled in those who value it enough to *pursue* it with the godly attitudes of reverence, humility, teachableness, diligence, uprightness, and faith (Proverbs 2:4-7; 9:9-10; 11:2; 15:31-33; 19:20; James 1:6).

While the quest for wisdom requires effort, it is never strictly academic. We gain wisdom through a partnership with God who engages with us hands-on. He mediates his wisdom through a variety of channels: the Bible, our own research, wise counselors, and the applied lessons of life (Nehemiah 2:11-16; Psalm 19:7; 119:97-100; Proverbs 6:6-11;

11:14; 13:20; 15:22; 30:24-28; Luke 1:3; 14:28-32; 2 Timothy 2:7; 3:15-17; 2 Peter 1:19). And as we practice wisdom in the experiences of life, we are *trained* in it (Hebrews 5:14).

Accordingly, the third principle of Christian decision making is: *Where there is no command, God gives us wisdom to choose.*

The Way of Wisdom

1. Where God commands, we must obey.
2. Where there is no command, God gives us freedom and responsibility to choose.
3. Where there is no command, God gives us wisdom to choose.

Don't Forget...

- The moral will of God consists of all the instructions, commands, and principles revealed by God in the Bible that teach us what to believe and how to live. Understanding and following the moral will of God is one of the most important components of decision making that is truly Christian.
- Marital decisions are non-commanded decisions. Rather than expecting God to tell you what to do, you are free and responsible to make wise choices (within moral limits).
- Wisdom should be sought from God through the variety of means he has provided.
- Three good test questions for evaluating options: (1) How can I best love God and man? (2) Which decision will best promote God's kingdom? and (3) How can I most skillfully serve God and his people?

To access the endnotes and for questions for reflection and group discussion go to:
www.TheMarriageDecision.com

Chapter 2

What in the World Is God Doing?

Julie was reeling. She had just returned home from bridesmaid's duty at her cousin's wedding—her fourth gig in as many years. She had occupied her mind on the plane ride by making mental notes on what *not* to do at her own wedding, should that ever materialize.

The first clue that something was amiss was Brad's embrace at the airport—it was less enthusiastic than she had been expecting. Stopping for coffee en route to her apartment, he delivered his prepared remarks. The company was fast-tracking him for management...East Coast...leaving next week...long-distance relationships don't work... not enough room for career and a family right now...not fair to her... blah, blah, blah.

No discussion, no debate, no negotiation. A fifteen-month investment cashed in with no return. At least he had been man enough to talk to her face-to-face without stringing her along, a bittersweet confirmation of his character.

When she was nineteen, Julie had read an essay being passed around the college dorm—"A Love Letter from Jesus." In it, Jesus promised that if she would devote herself to him, find her soul's satisfaction in him, at the right time, when she was ready, he would bring into her life "the one I have for you." The letter struck her even then as a sentimental fantasy, but it seemed to flesh out the promise of Psalm 37:4 (ESV): "Delight yourself in the LORD, and he will give you the desires of your heart." So, for a decade, she had followed the prescription to the best of her ability. Her next birthday would begin with the number three, and the best, latest candidate for "the one" had just driven off into the night.

Was she missing something? What in the world was God doing?

* * * * * * * *

Like Julie, the apostle Paul had a fervent desire that was being blocked by circumstances beyond his control. Situated in Corinth, he wanted to take his gospel ministry west to Rome, and beyond. But more pressing concerns were interfering with his plans. However, unlike Julie, he was not exasperated by disappointing reversals. That's because he was aware that another plan was being worked out—one that took precedence over his own and, perhaps, might include elements of his strategy.

This is how he explained his perspective to the Roman Christians:

> God...is my witness that I continually remember you and I always ask in my prayers, if perhaps now at last I may succeed in visiting you *according to the will of God*. For I long to see you, so that I may impart to you some spiritual gift to strengthen you, that is, that we may be mutually comforted by one another's faith, both yours and mine. I do not want you to be unaware, brothers and sisters, that I often intended to come to you (*and was prevented until now*), so that I may have some fruit even among you, just as I already have among the rest of the Gentiles (Romans 1:9-13).

In contrast to the recorded instances in which God told Paul specifically what to do (such as the Macedonian Call in Acts 16:9-10), Paul's determination to visit Rome was not dictated by God. The idea for the visit emerged as Paul was developing long-term ministry goals. So he approached the decision-making process the same way he did other non-commanded decisions. First, he adopted spiritual objectives that were based on God's moral will. Next, he devised plans that gave him a strategy for accomplishing his goals.[1] And throughout the process, his planning was accompanied by prayer.

But even as Paul was making his plans, he knew another dynamic was at work. This is evident in his prayer that "now at last I may succeed in visiting you *according to the will of God*." What Paul understood is that his efforts to get to Rome would succeed only if his plans were in harmony with and brought to fulfillment by God's *sovereign* will.[2]

By way of definition, the sovereign will is *God's secret plan that determines everything that happens in the universe.*[3] God's sovereign will is distinct from (though related to) his moral will. God's moral will concerns what he wants the believer to do; his sovereign will is what he himself is doing. God's moral will is prescribed; his sovereign will is hidden.

Paul understood that the stories of our lives unfold along two tracks.

- The one is visible; the other is hidden.
- The one concerns our decision making and actions as we play out our roles; the other concerns the work of God behind the scenes to bring about his purposes.
- The one presumes our freedom to make real decisions; the other takes for granted God's sovereign control over all things, including our choices.

In the previous chapter, I unpacked the first three principles in God's design for decision making.

THE WAY OF WISDOM

1. Where God commands, we must obey.
2. Where there is no command, God gives us freedom and responsibility to choose.
3. Where there is no command, God gives us wisdom to choose.

A fourth principle emerges from the believer's response to the reality of God's sovereign will: *When we have chosen what is moral and wise, we must trust the sovereign God to work all the details together for good.*

The Nature of God's Sovereign Will

When human beings attempt to grasp how God implements his sovereign will, we are confronted with genuine mystery. For the doctrine of God's sovereignty takes us beyond the limits of our human comprehension, and our intellectual tensions are not resolved for us by the biblical writers.[4] Nevertheless, Christian decision makers need to recognize what is revealed about God's sovereign will in Scripture. Then we will be in position to appreciate how biblical characters and writers responded to it as they sought to honor God with their decisions.

In this brief survey, we affirm five things about God's sovereign will.[5]

First, it is certain of fulfillment. If God decrees something, it will happen. There is no force in the universe that can frustrate his will (Daniel 4:34-35; Acts 2:23; 4:27-28; Romans 9:6-29).

Second, God's sovereign will is detailed—it encompasses all things. It will ultimately determine the outcome of our plans, the existence of creation, a king's decisions, the result of rolled dice, the believer's experience of suffering, and our personal salvation (James 4:13-15; Revelation 4:11; Proverbs 16:33; 21:1; 1 Peter 3:17; Romans 8:29-30; 2 Thessalonians 2:13-14). In a word, the sovereign God "accomplishes *all things* according to the counsel of his will" (Ephesians 1:11).

Third, God's sovereign will is hidden. "Secret things belong to the LORD our God" (Deuteronomy 29:29). Older theologians often referred to God's sovereign will as His "secret will," in contrast to his revealed will in the Bible. God hides his sovereign will until it happens.[6]

Fourth, God's sovereign will is the supreme determiner of all things without violating human responsibility or making God the author of sin.

The revelation concerning God's sovereign will creates tensions in our minds with other biblical teachings.[7] In the context of decision making, we encounter two glaring puzzles: If God sovereignly determines everything that happens, how can human decisions have any meaning? And what about the bad things that happen? Doesn't this teaching on sovereignty make God responsible for sin?

God's Sovereignty and Human Decisions

These are complex philosophical issues that merit more consideration than we can give here. But two observations have been helpful to me. The first is that biblical writers do not subscribe to the logic behind our questions. They affirm both sides of each assertion without making any attempt to resolve them. They assert that human beings are moral agents who make real decisions for which they are responsible, and they maintain that God is sovereignly in control of all things. They establish the culpability of evil behavior on the part of sinful men and women, and they hold that God is righteous in all he does (Psalm 145:17; James 1:13). Without apology, without explanation, without any effort to remove the tension, God's sovereignty and man's responsibility are sometimes asserted side by side in Scripture (Matthew 26:14-16,24; Luke 22:21-22; Acts 2:22-23; 4:27-28; Romans 9:6-29).

The second observation is that when we reach the limits of our comprehension, God often directs our attention away from our philosophical perplexities (which one day will be resolved—1 Corinthians 13:11-12) to the cross. For there we see the ultimate instance of God's sovereign will brought about by wicked humanity.

One statement, declared by Simon Peter in his Pentecost sermon, epitomizes the Bible's handling of these seemingly contradictory ideas: "Jesus the Nazarene...who was handed over by the predetermined plan and foreknowledge of God, you executed by nailing him to a cross at the hands of Gentiles" (Act 2:22-23). Peter holds his audience responsible and accountable for their complicity in the crucifixion of Jesus, while affirming that God had predetermined that very event. The most heinous crime in human history—the willful murder of the Son of God, Israel's Messiah—actually accomplished the central requirement in God's glorious plan of redemption. If the worst thing that ever happened could also be the best thing that ever happened, everything else is a footnote.

And so, as we exercise our freedom and responsibility to make choices, God, by his Spirit, is himself engaged. And his activity is not only parallel to our own, but he is at work ahead of, behind, around, over, under, and through us. Our own behaviors and choices are governed by his sovereign will. And yet, God is not a Cosmic Puppeteer, and we are not marionettes that jump when he jerks our strings. No one can excuse his (mis)behavior with the assertion, "God made me do it," or even "The devil made me do it." A person's decision constitutes a real cause, produces genuine effects, and brings accountability. God is the ultimate determiner, but humans produce real secondary causes with their decisions and actions.

God's Sovereignty and Life's Difficulties

Wrestling with this mystery gives me a headache. But it also serves the useful purpose of pointing to the *fifth characteristic of God's sovereign will: it is good.* "And we know that all things work together *for good* for those who love God, who are called according to his purpose" (Romans 8:28).

When we read this verse, we must have a grown-up conception of *good*. The goodness that characterizes the sovereign will of God is good because it accomplishes his good purposes and ultimately brings the greatest glory to him (Ephesians 1:3-14; Romans 11:30-33). Romans 8:28 does not say that all things *are* good, for they are not. Rather, all things *work together* for good.

This is an important concept for single adults who face marital decisions. One of the reasons individuals wish that God would tell them what to do is that such decisions would then be "perfect." If God were to choose my spouse, she would be ideally suited for me (and I for her). We would be true soul mates and we would live happily ever after. I call this "Disney theology." A moment's reflection should expose this idea as a fantasy. (Are you *really* ideally suited for anyone else?) God's approach treats us as adults who live in a real, though fallen, world.

Here's the wonder of God's sovereign will: often our experience of the hard things of life leads to the accomplishment of what is truly good. That truth is clearly illustrated in the story of Joseph narrated in Genesis 37–50.

Because God gave Joseph the ability to interpret divinely transmitted dreams, Joseph gave Pharaoh the information he needed to avert a major famine. But the journey that brought Joseph to the pinnacle of power was anything but easy.

To get from the pasturelands of Canaan to the court of Pharaoh, Joseph was required to experience reversals and the anguish of unfair treatment from people who should have been on his side. There is no indication that he ever violated the moral will of God. He seemed to get punished, repeatedly, for persisting in doing the right thing. And then, almost overnight, he rocketed from the nadir of prison to the apex of power and authority. And he changed history—and preserved the messianic line.

In a final confrontation with his brothers Joseph gave his explanation for the downs and ups of his remarkable career: "As for you, you meant to harm me, but God intended it for a good purpose, so he could preserve the lives of many people, as you can see this day" (Genesis 50:20).

Not only does sin not negate the sovereign will of God, he actually uses sinful people and difficult experiences (including those problems we bring on ourselves) to produce good outcomes—when we respond properly.

This is a persistent theme of Scripture (Acts 14:21-22; Romans 5:1-5; 2 Corinthians 12:7-10; James 1:2-6; 1 Peter 1:3-9; 2:19-24; 3:13-17; 4:12-19; Hebrews 10:32-39; 11:32–12:14). The hardships we encounter as a result of living in a fallen world can be used by God to produce at least three benefits:

1. We gain a deeper experience of God's presence and grace that comes from greater dependence upon him (because of our need).
2. We grow in spiritual character as we are cured of our self-centeredness and become more like Christ.
3. Through the process of healing and growth, we become equipped to minister to others who experience similar difficulties.

These are all good purposes that can be accomplished by God's sovereign will.

This does not mean we will always recognize God's good purposes in our difficulties. All of our why questions ultimately must have the same answer—our loving God in his sovereign wisdom willed it so. Os Guinness has wisely observed: "As believers we cannot always know why, but *we can always know why we trust God who knows why*, and this makes all the difference."[8]

Will Julie, who felt rejected by Brad and let down by God, believe in the goodness of a plan that has produced such disappointment and pain? We know how Joseph's circumstances were providentially reversed for the better. And we can see how his earlier challenges helped to prepare him for his ultimate opportunity. But why should Julie believe that God's long-term plan is better than the one she had been hoping for with Brad?

The Bible's answer is simple and brief: "Indeed, he who did not spare his own Son, but gave him up for us all—how will he not also, along with him, freely give us all things?" (Romans 8:32). God has already given us the Greatest Gift, solved our Deepest Problem, paid the Dearest Price in providing our salvation. In the gracious offering of his Son, God has demonstrated the reality of his goodness overwhelmingly. He could scarcely be good in providing the Big Thing and fail to be good in the little matters of our lives. What he chooses to give us "along with him" will be good.

In *Knowing God*, J.I. Packer spells out the stunning implications of Romans 8:32:

> Paul is telling us that there is no ultimate loss or irreparable impoverishment to be feared; if God denies us something, it is only in order to make room for one or another of the things He has in mind...The meaning of "He will give us all things" can be put thus: one day we shall see that nothing—literally nothing—that could have increased our eternal happiness has been denied us, and that nothing—literally nothing—that could have reduced that happiness has been left with us. What higher assurance do we want than that?[9]

God's Sovereign Will
At-a-Glance

It is certain of fulfillment

It is detailed—including all things

It is hidden—it cannot be known in advance

It is supreme—without violating human responsibility or making God the author of sin

It is good—working all things together for God's glory and our good

Here, then, is the essence of the Way of Wisdom: *Christians are called to make wise decisions within the moral will of God, trusting in the sovereign will of God to accomplish his good purposes in and through us.*

As we turn our attention to God's design for singleness, we will see how Jesus and Paul apply these principles to marital decision making.

Don't Forget...

- While the Christian exercises his freedom and responsibility to make wise decisions within God's moral will, God is at work behind the scenes to bring about his sovereign will.
- God's sovereign will is certain, detailed, hidden, supreme, and good.
- The experience of God's sovereign will in our lives is not always pleasant. But our difficulties often lead to the accomplishment of what is truly good.

To access the endnotes and for questions for reflection and group discussion go to:

www.TheMarriageDecision.com

PART 2

God's Design for Singleness

MODERN MYTH 2

Singleness should be regarded as a transitional state en route to the ultimate destination of marriage. Problems stemming from the incompleteness of singleness are resolved by marriage.

Introduction to Part 2

God's Design for Singleness

Nancy was grading papers on the dining room table when she overheard her mother talking on the phone in the kitchen: "Honestly, Fran, I don't think I'm ever going to have grandchildren."

Nancy sighed. She tried to visit her parents as often as possible, but she had to brace herself for the comments she could expect. Her mother meant well. In her efforts to prod Nancy into taking action to find a husband, Mom tried to avoid nagging. But her exasperation was thinly disguised. "At least find a church singles group that has some men in it." And it only added to Nancy's frustration.

When she graduated from high school, Nancy had a scenario in her mind about how her life was going to play out. The first order of business was college. She would take the coursework required to get her teaching certificate. As opportunities arose, she would pursue adventures in travel and short-term missions work. Somewhere along the line, she would meet Mr. Right and marriage would ensue. Children would be born and a family would begin to grow. Within that same timeframe, careers would be launched and the responsibilities of adult living would be assumed.

The first part of the story line unfolded nicely, accompanied by "Someday My Prince Will Come." As she played her part, she waited for the hero to make his entrance. But he never showed. He missed her graduation, her certification, her first teaching job. And now that she was out of school, not only did he remain AWOL, but the opportunities for her to even meet a potential husband had dwindled from slim to none—a fact of life italicized by her mother's panicky urgings.

As she invested heavily in the lives of children who were not her own, she acknowledged that the desire to marry and have a family was still there. It was something she had prayed for and continued to pray for. And yet, three years into a job that was starting to look like a profession, she found that she was adapting, coming to terms with the possibility that real life might deviate from the long-held master plan.

What she found surprising, and frustrating, was that it was proving easier to loosen her grip on her aspirations than it was to deal with the expectations of others. Her mother was hardly a lone voice. Mom was the ever-present incarnation of everyone in her extended family—and her spiritual family. Tactful friends had stopped addressing her singleness directly. But still, everywhere she turned, she encountered The Question. Less sensitive folks framed it in the guise of a joke, but more often she read it in people's eyes: *What's wrong with you? When are you going to get married?*

Nancy had lots of evidence that she was a highly capable woman who was making a significant contribution with her life and who, if it came to that, would make someone a wonderful wife. And yet she couldn't help but wonder: *Is something wrong with me? And if that's true, what am I supposed to do about it?*

••••••••

A lot of people get married. But everyone starts out single. And well over half of those who get married spend some segment of their adult lives single again. In today's world, *single* is the primary adjective describing significant stages in the life of an adult. In fact, we happen to live at a juncture in history where, for the first time, the number of single adults in America is almost equal to, and may soon surpass, the number of married adults.[1]

This demographic curiosity notwithstanding, singles are obliged to navigate life in a world more oriented toward married couples and households with children. This is especially true in the social environment of the church with its prevailing focus on the family. While single adults are technically a part of this spiritual family, when it comes to ministry and fellowship, they find they are often, literally, the odd man out.

Albert Hsu addresses this in his book *Singles at the Crossroads*:

> The marriage books [in Christian bookstores] never argue that marriage is a good thing. That is presupposed. They accept the reality that marriages often have problems, so that's what these marriage books are for: dealing with the problems. But books on singleness usually have a different approach. Instead of dealing with problems that singles might face, these books seem to think singleness *is* the problem. They instruct the reader on how to bide one's time until the right person comes along. In other words, they imply that the one solution to the problem of singleness is to get married. Then one can have marriage problems and read all those marriage books.[2]

In *Women in the Maze*, Ruth Tucker suggests we may have inherited this perspective from the leaders of the Reformation: "We [Protestants] view the emphasis on celibacy[3] in the Roman Catholic church as misdirected, and we can see the problems that have resulted from it. But it is entirely possible that we have gone to the other extreme, so that subconsciously we view singles as somehow defective."[4]

Second-Class Singles?

Our second modern myth—that singleness is to be viewed as a temporary condition, a transitional stage en route to the ultimate destination of marriage—is widely accepted within the evangelical subculture. And it is shared to a considerable degree by unmarried people themselves. The nearly universal scope of this viewpoint is not difficult to understand, for it is reinforced by several supporting factors.

First, we are collectively under the impression that while the Bible speaks favorably of marriage, it treats singleness as, well, undesirable. At weddings, especially, we often read this passage from Ecclesiastes 4:9-11:

Two people are better than one,
 because they can reap more benefit from their labor.
For if they fall, one will help his companion up,
 but pity the person who falls down and has no one to help him up.
Furthermore, if two lie down together, they can keep each other warm,
 but how can one person keep warm by himself?

In sermons from Genesis 2, preachers drive home the point that while the first man started out as a bachelor, his status was "not good" and, hence, temporary. In part 3 of this book, I will make the point that Adam was incomplete by design. He needed a helper. So God gave him a spouse. Marriage was created to be the norm[5] and, though the institution has been corrupted by the fall, a Spirit-filled marriage is a great blessing—a picture, even, of Christ and his church (Ephesians 5:22-33). In the face of this, it is hard to escape the conclusion that the single journey is destined to find its fulfillment in marriage.

The inclination to adopt this perception is further motivated by the intense desire on the part of the unmarried person—produced by the combination of his or her biological makeup and a yearning for the blessings of a healthy marriage—to get married. This desire easily morphs into an *expectation* that a husband or wife will prove to be God's fulfillment of his promise to grant Christian singles the desires of their hearts (Psalm 37:4).

And it seems to work out that way for many people. The idea that everyone who truly wants to get married will do so is reinforced by the statistic that, historically, most adults do marry. At least so far.

And yet there are two serious flaws with the notion that singleness finds its fulfilling destination only in marriage. The first is that this universal expectation can produce adverse effects in the lives of single persons. We've already seen this in Nancy's case. The consistent message from her community is that her continued singleness means something's wrong with her—and she's beginning to wonder if they're right. This kind of pressure has prompted some individuals to enter into an ill-advised marriage.

Now it is bad enough when one unmarried person suffers from the widespread perception that they are somehow defective. But when the impact of this assumption is multiplied across the lives of the growing number of single adults among us, the harmful effects of the "marriage expectation" are compounded:

- It consigns single adults to second-class status within the family of Christ.
- It makes marriage the only rite of passage for acknowledging adulthood.
- It fans a legitimate desire into a demand.
- When the expectation is not fulfilled, it intensifies disappointment and raises the question of blame, casting aspersions on the worthiness of the individual and the goodness of God.

After a while, being on the receiving end of this kind of "encouragement" prompts single Christians to distance themselves from their well-meaning Job's comforters. This myth actually drives a wedge between single Christians and their married counterparts, hampering fellowship within the body of Christ.

Such detrimental consequences should be a clue that our accepted viewpoint is out of sync with God's design. And that is, in fact, the second flaw. *The good news is that we have been wrong.* We have inflated a widespread pattern into a universal one—taking what is commonly desired and frequently experienced and making it *normative* for everyone—without biblical warrant. And we have overlooked important biblical instruction on singleness that would give us a more balanced perspective. The pervasive view that singleness is inferior to marriage flies in the face of the teaching (to say nothing of the example) of both Jesus and Paul.

As we will see in the following pages, Jesus not only redefined the role of marriage in a fallen world, he also elevated the status of singleness to a place of significance equal to that of marriage within the family of God. And Paul, the apostle who revealed to the church the mystery that Spirit-filled marriage portrays the relationship between Christ and his bride, actively *recruited* unmarried Christians in Corinth to remain single!

....

I'm going to let you in on a secret. It hasn't been easy for me to communicate to others, in advance, what this book is about. Because of the assumptions I've been discussing, many potential readers probably think this book represents one more attempt to help single people solve their problem by helping them to get married. That is not the case.

Having read this far, you may now wonder if I'm about to try to talk singles out of their desire for marriage. That is not the case either.

What we are about to see is that just as God has a design for marriage, he also has a design for singleness. My hope is that readers who are single will not seek marriage simply as an escape from singleness. Rather, I hope they will appreciate and embrace God's design for singleness for as long as they remain single. That will be the best preparation for whatever lies ahead in the sovereign will of God—whether one marries or remains single.

....

To access the endnotes and for questions for reflection
and group discussion go to:

www.TheMarriageDecision.com

Chapter 3

Jesus: Singleness Is Just as Honorable as Marriage

When Jesus launched his public ministry, he rocked his world. *Amazed* is the word the authors of the Gospels use to describe the reaction of the people (Matthew 7:28; 21:20; Mark 1:22,27; 12:17; Luke 9:43; 11:14; John 3:7; 4:27). They were astounded by his teaching, his authority, his power. But one other thing about Jesus that the chroniclers scarcely mention must have been striking to his contemporaries:

Jesus never married.

He chose to remain single in a culture that was far more committed to marriage than the contemporary church is. And his determination to carry out his ministry as a single man was the first flare fired across the bow of Jewish society, signaling a major shift in God's intent for marriage and singleness in a fallen world.

No Place for Singles

In the beginning, prior to the Rebellion, marriage was the only human social institution. In the generations that followed, it retained a central place in the structure of societies as the nuclear family expanded into an extended family, and then into clans, tribes, and nations. Israelite culture, in particular, was organized around family clans, so marriage and children played a key role. In fact, Jewish couples had a double-duty to procreate.

Their first obligation was personal—they needed children to

provide for them in their old age and to preserve their legacy when they died. So the propagation of each *family* line was of paramount importance. To not get married would be catastrophic because it would leave one without heirs and effectively delete one's name from the collective memory of the nation.

The second concern was corporate—the shared responsibility to perpetuate the *messianic* line. From the time God promised Abraham that he would bless the world through his offspring, the people of God were biologically defined. The advancement of the kingdom and the maintenance of the messianic hope occurred through physical procreation. Accordingly, Israelite men and women were virtually *obligated to marry* and beget children. The genealogical record the New Testament opens with (Matthew 1:1-17) underscores the significance of the family connections through which God's covenant was maintained.

As a result, there was virtually no place for single adults in Hebrew culture. In fact, there is no word for *bachelor* in the Old Testament.[1]

But when the One who fulfilled the promises to Abraham arrived, and the messianic goal to which generations of Jewish couples had contributed was accomplished, things began to change. And Jesus's abstention from marriage was a stunning first clue that the nature of one's marital status in God's social order was under reconstruction.

Singleness: An Alternative Path

This change was signaled not only by Jesus's aberrant lifestyle but also by his teaching. One of his most provocative statements was made in the context of an encounter with some religious opponents.

> Then some Pharisees came to him in order to test him. They asked, "Is it lawful to divorce a wife for any cause?" He answered, "Have you not read that from the beginning the Creator 'made them male and female,' and said, 'For this reason a man will leave his father and mother and will be united with his wife, and the two will become one flesh'? So they are no longer two, but one flesh. Therefore what God has joined together, let no one separate." They said to him, "Why then did Moses command us 'to give

> a certificate of dismissal' and to divorce her?" Jesus said to them, "Moses permitted you to divorce your wives because of your hard hearts, but from the beginning it was not this way. Now I say to you that whoever divorces his wife, except for immorality, and marries another commits adultery" (Matthew 19:3-9).

Jesus's disciples, who were often a little slow on the uptake, immediately grasped the implications of this pronouncement: "If this is the case of a husband with a wife, it is better not to marry!" (19:10). If divorce was ruled out except for immorality, a man could be permanently locked into an intolerable situation.

Jesus's reply served notice, once again, that a new day was dawning. What he actually said was:

> "Not everyone can accept this statement, except those to whom it has been given. For there are some eunuchs who were that way from birth, and some who were made eunuchs by others, and some who became eunuchs for the sake of the kingdom of heaven. The one who is able to accept this should accept it" (Matthew 19:11-12).

Jesus's response to his disciples was startling at several levels. I'm guessing that the disciples weren't expecting Jesus to agree with their conclusion. But he did. When he said, "some became eunuchs[2] for the sake of the kingdom of heaven," he was affirming that it is better for *some* not to marry. This assertion contradicted the orthodox party line, as we have seen. Not only did the rabbis insist that it was the duty for every Israelite to marry, they were themselves married. Both in his practice and in his teaching, Jesus was an anomaly.

But Jesus corrected his disciples' *reason* for considering a single life. Rather than a negative fear of imprisonment in a miserable marriage, Jesus advanced a constructive reason: "for the sake of the kingdom of heaven." Just as Jesus's freedom from the obligations of marriage enabled him to focus on his messianic task, so some of his followers would choose to follow his example in order to advance his kingdom.

The men Jesus was speaking to, being Jewish, were accustomed to think of marriage as obligatory. Being married themselves, they knew how difficult it was to log in so much time with Jesus and manage their family responsibilities as well. The preceding debate had focused on the ethics of terminating a marriage by means of divorce—an option Jesus essentially disallowed. But he *was* suggesting a radical alternative for future disciples—some could choose to not get married in the first place (just as the disciples said).[3]

It probably took them a while to get it, but Jesus was dramatically reordering not only his disciples' perspective but their priorities. First, he was underscoring that the kingdom of heaven—the kingdom to which he had challenged them to give their highest devotion (Matthew 6:33)—was more important than one's marital status. Second, in a culture where marriage was compulsory, Jesus was sanctioning an alternative path for kingdom service. And third, he was strongly implying that a disciple's marital choices should be evaluated on the basis of the potential for those choices to advance the rule of God.

Eunuchs? What's With That?

There is, of course, a cost attached to this expression of commitment to Christ's kingdom. The disciple who chooses a life of singleness forfeits the benefits of marriage—specifically the children who comprise their parents' social security system and the extension of the family line. And so we might expect the question to arise: How could anyone afford to pay that high a price?[4]

The answer may have been suggested by Jesus's striking use of *eunuchs* to refer to those who choose not to marry. That term may cause modern readers to wince because it refers to men who have been castrated—a circumstance we'd rather not think about. But in the Jewish culture of the first century, the misfortune experienced by eunuchs went far beyond the condition of impotence and the loss of potential offspring. They were barred from participation in the worship experiences of the Israelite community (Deuteronomy 23:1). In a society that had no place for singles, they *were* the singles. Viewed through the lens of legalism, they were widely regarded as social lepers.

But Jews who knew their way around the Hebrew Bible would also be aware of a remarkable passage that describes some of the changes that will occur in the coming day of deliverance. In Isaiah 56:3-5 (ESV), the Lord says,

> Let not the foreigner who has joined himself to the LORD
> say,
> "The LORD will surely separate me from his people";
> and let not the eunuch say,
> "Behold, I am a dry tree."
> For thus says the LORD:
> "To the eunuchs who keep my Sabbaths,
> who choose the things that please me
> and hold fast my covenant,
> I will give in my house and within my walls
> a monument and a name
> better than sons and daughters;
> I will give them an everlasting name
> that shall not be cut off."

From the perspective of Isaiah, in a future time eunuchs who were faithful to God's covenant would receive blessing from God in the form of an "everlasting name" that "is better than sons and daughters" and "shall not be cut off." During the Old Covenant, the only way a man's name could be perpetuated ("not cut off") was through physical procreation. But that was impossible for eunuchs. So how could this promise be fulfilled? How could eunuchs acquire such a legacy?

It turns out there is more than one way to beget children. Consider another verse from the famous description of Messiah in Isaiah 53:

> Yet it was the will of the LORD to crush him;
> he has put him to grief;
> when his soul makes an offering for guilt,
> *he shall see his offspring*; he shall prolong his days;
> the will of the LORD shall prosper in his hand.
> (Isaiah 53:10 ESV, italics added)

This passage, as we know, was describing Jesus—a celibate man. In what sense did he produce offspring through his death and resurrection? This has to be referring to his spiritual children—the "family" of Christ, the church that is born in the New Testament. This is that family that Jesus himself referred to in Matthew 12:49-50—those who "do the will of my Father in heaven." This is that family that comes into being not through physical procreation but through new birth by faith (John 1:11-13).

If Jesus had Isaiah's prophecy in mind in the eunuch statements of Matthew 19:11-12, he would be implying that the day foretold by Isaiah had arrived. And that those "eunuchs" who choose to forego marriage for the sake of the kingdom of heaven contribute to the birth of spiritual offspring[5]—a mission, and a blessing, greater than the physical begetting of sons and daughters. In this way, at least, "Eunuchs for Yeshua" are given the honor of "an everlasting name that shall not be cut off."

So when Peter asked Jesus point blank whether the sacrifices he and others had made to follow him would prove to be worth it, Jesus said, "I tell you the truth, there is no one who has left home or wife or brothers or parents or children for the sake of God's kingdom who will not receive many times more in this age—and in the age to come, eternal life" (Luke 18:28-30).

No longer were Jesus's disciples to conceive of God's kingdom primarily as an earthly realm in Palestine ruled by a descendent of King David and populated by Israelite families (Acts 1:6-8). No longer were they to rely on their physical progeny to provide their long-term security and permanent significance in the annals of history. Timothy and Kathy Keller underscore this idea in *The Meaning of Marriage*:

> Single adult Christians were bearing testimony that God, not family, was their hope. God would guarantee their future, first by giving them their truest family—the church—so they never lacked for brothers and sisters, fathers and mothers, in Christ. But ultimately, Christians' inheritance is nothing less than the fullness of the kingdom of God in the new heavens and the new earth.[6]

And the Point Is...

Now, what relevance does the teaching of King Jesus have for contemporary singles who are being told that singleness should be regarded as a transitional state en route to the ultimate destination of marriage?

First, by virtue of his precedent in foregoing marriage and his striking pronouncement exempting some disciples from marital obligations, *Jesus elevated singleness to the same level of legitimacy as marriage.* Unmarried disciples who are investing their lives in the kingdom of God do not have to get married to have a place of value and honor in the community of faith.

And so, the experience of singleness should not be reduced to a time of preparation for marriage. It should rather been seen as a platform of great opportunity for the advancement of the kingdom of God. If singleness is a stage of life, it ought to be viewed as preparatory for *whatever comes next* in the sovereign will of God—whether marriage or continued singleness. And far from waiting for marriage to get on with life, single Christians should maximize the potential of their state for growing in their devotion to God and serving him for so long as they are single.

Second, Jesus added a new factor for single adults to consider in marital decision making—namely, the impact of their marital status on their contribution to the kingdom of God.

Finally, this whole approach to marital decision making requires a radically different way of thinking. In the introduction to part 1 ("God's Design for Decision Making"), I began to describe how Christians approach their choices differently from everyone else. Now we need to add one more distinctive: Jesus's disciples *take the long view.* This business of "begetting spiritual offspring" and "inheriting an everlasting name" will gain no traction apart from an eternal perspective.

First-century Israelites and modern-day secularists share a severely limited, short-sighted vision of human life span. Christians who see clearly view this present life as a prelude to the age to come—a foreshadowing of the real life that lies ahead (2 Corinthians 4:16-18). Remarkably, we are given the opportunity to make significant investments in what is eternal by means of our service to Christ in this life (Matthew 6:19-21). Jesus fully expects that this expanded frame of reference will shape our choices in the present.

Perhaps you have accepted the idea of eternal destiny as a tenet of your Christian faith, but until now you haven't seen its relevance for decision making in the present. You will have to decide whether your *belief* is going to operate at the level of *conviction*. For that to happen, you must have strong reasons for confidence in the promise of our eternal hope. For me, the clincher is the historical, bodily resurrection of Jesus from the dead. That was also the clincher for Simon Peter. The same man who asked Jesus, "What's in it for us?" shared his own conviction toward the end of his life:

> Blessed be the God and Father of our Lord Jesus Christ! By his great mercy he gave us new birth into a living hope through the resurrection of Jesus Christ from the dead, that is, into an inheritance imperishable, undefiled, and unfading. It is reserved in heaven for you (1 Peter 1:3-4).

Though we live in a fallen world, Jesus came to give us abundant life in the present (John 10:10). But we don't have to have it all now—because we will have it all, and more, when we get home (1 Corinthians 2:9). It's already in the Bank.

Don't Forget...

- Jesus elevated the status of singleness to the same level of legitimacy and honor as marriage.
- Singleness should be viewed as a platform of great opportunity for advancing the kingdom of God.
- As a stage of life, singleness is preparatory for whatever comes next in the sovereign will of God—whether marriage or continued singleness.
- Christians who seize the ministry opportunities afforded

by their single status to advance God's kingdom are making an investment in an inheritance that is eternal.

To access the endnotes and for questions for reflection and group discussion go to:

www.TheMarriageDecision.com

Chapter 4

Paul: Singleness Is (Sometimes) Better than Marriage

Until Jesus brought it up, it doesn't look like anyone in the Jewish culture had seriously considered bachelorhood an option. Then when he put the idea out there, it may have sounded as if he were contrasting two acceptable options—a *lifetime* of celibacy versus a *lifetime* of marriage. Choose one or the other.

I don't think that's how most singles living today frame the issues. To begin with, single people don't *choose* singleness—it's how they start out. It's their default condition. So the issue isn't strictly a choice between singleness and marriage but whether there is going to be a *change* of marital status. The question becomes: Shall I *remain* single or shall I get married?

But that's not how the question presents itself either. For while a person can remain single without doing anything, they can't just choose the alternative and then go do it. Marriage, as an option, is initially theoretical.

People who eventually marry usually go through three broad stages in the decision-making process. The starting point is the state of being *not ready for marriage*. For most people this begins the day they turn eighteen and become legally of age. Unless they happen to be terminally in love on that date, most who are technically eligible for marriage have other priorities for the first few years of young adulthood.

This status changes when one becomes *available for marriage*. It might begin with something as simple as flipping a mental switch from "not interested" to "I think I'm in the market." And the level of energy invested could range from attending functions frequented by members of the opposite sex to a fairly aggressive marketing campaign.

There's a nuance to these first two stages that must not be missed. The initial position, "not interested," does not usually mean, "I want to be single forever." More often it means, "It is better for me to be single *at the moment*." Like Nancy the schoolteacher, most single people expect to get married someday. It's not so much a choice as an assumption. So the first engagement with the process is more about when than whether. It's a decision to get into the game.

The third stage is activated when *a live candidate emerges*. Falling in love dramatically alters the dynamics. But again, the decision at this point isn't so much about choosing between singleness and marriage but rather, "Is *this* person the one and is *now* the time?"

Of course, the trajectory between singleness and marriage is seldom a straight line. Some people, like Nancy, seem to get stranded in stage two. Others cycle back and forth from one stage to the other—as when the answer to the question, "Is this the one?" turns out to be, "No, keep looking."

So when Nancy's supposed encouragers inquire, "Why don't you get married?" she wants to say, "Hey, it's not that easy." We're not talking about three simple steps to the altar. Many intermediate choices have to be made along the way. Also, other people get to cast votes (or exercise vetoes) that have a way of affecting one's options.

No, it's not that simple. And so far we've considered only the human side of the equation. In chapter 2 we learned that the ultimate determiner of our destiny is the sovereign will of God. *How does that factor into the mix?* we wonder.

The Implications of Jesus's Teaching for Marital Decision Making

Right about now someone needs to raise their hand and ask, "Is there any place in the Bible that addresses this specific decision-making process?"

Happily, the answer is yes—1 Corinthians 7. What Jesus mentioned cryptically in a single verse, Paul expounded for an entire chapter. What Paul wrote amounts to a commentary on the implications of Jesus's teaching for marital decision making.

(My personal exposition of 1 Corinthians 7, and the principles that emerge from that text, are published in chapters 8 and 9 of *Singleness, Marriage, and the Will of God.* In this edition, I am aiming to share enough of that material to make sense of the conclusions without getting bogged down in an overly technical discussion.[1] As you read the remainder of this chapter, it would be a good idea to have a Bible nearby, open to 1 Corinthians 7.)

Corinthian Questions

The members of the Corinthian church had not been believers in Jesus for very long. They had turned to Christ from a background of Greco-Roman paganism. And they were having a difficult time understanding and applying the implications of the gospel in ways that produced godly living. The book of 1 Corinthians was a letter the apostle Paul wrote to these believers to address problems that had arisen within that group (chapters 1–6) and to answer questions submitted to him by the church's leaders (chapters 7–16).

The seventh chapter is kind of like a blog that Paul wrote in answer to questions about sexuality, marriage, and singleness. Paul introduces his comments this way: "Now concerning the things of which you wrote to me: It is good for a man not to touch a woman" (7:1 NKJV).

Most commentators believe that the statement about "not touching a woman" was a direct quote from the Corinthian inquirers, and that *touch* was a euphemism for sexual relations.[2] Standing behind this initial query was likely a host of questions concerning the ways in which Christians could maintain sexual purity in the variety of circumstances they found themselves in. Was it necessary for believers to make changes in their marital relationships in order to avoid the sin of sexual immorality?

Paul's Message

Paul's blog covered terrain spanning forty verses. But all of his counsel—to married couples, widow(er)s, divorcé(e)s, and never-married singles—was an elaboration of a single spiritual principle applied through one practical guideline. The principle is succinctly stated in 7:35; the guideline is spelled out in the central paragraph, 7:17-24, which also provides additional illustrations of the governing principle.

- *Principle*: Make the most of every circumstance to maximize your service and devotion to the Lord.
- *Guideline*: "Remain as you are" (7:17,20,24). That is, rather than take dramatic steps to change one's status—whether ethnic, social, or marital[3]—the believer should first learn how to live out his vocation as a disciple of Christ in the life situation he was in at the time of conversion.

The manner in which Paul's counsel was applied would vary with the diverse circumstances of the church members. So he spelled out the ramifications for *every marital situation* represented in the Corinthian congregation. Here is a summary of what he said.[4]

---

1 CORINTHIANS 7

Part 1: Counsel to the Married and Previously Married (1-16)

A. For the married: *Maintain sexual relations* (1-7).

B. For widowers and widows: *Stay unmarried, unless you can't handle it* (8-9).

C. For Christian married couples: *No divorce* (10-11).

D. For Christians married to unbelievers: *Stay in the marriage* (12-16).

Part 2: General Rule: *Remain as You Were When Called* (17-24)

Part 3: Counsel to the Never-Married and Widowed (25-40)

A. For the never-married: *Remain as you are* (25-38).

B. For widows: *Remarriage permitted, though happier unmarried* (39-40).

The Way of Wisdom

First Corinthians 7 contains more apostolic instruction for single Christians considering marriage than any other passage in the Bible. And one of the most striking things about this text is what it does *not* say. At no point in this chapter (or anywhere else) does Paul direct unmarried believers to ask God to tell them what they should do. Paul appears to be completely ignorant of every aspect of the teaching on guidance that Tom and Sandee received.

What he did say in this passage about decision making is so clear and comprehensive, it provides solid substantiation for every component of the Way of Wisdom. By way of review, here are the four principles Paul applies to all of our choices

---

The Way of Wisdom

1. Where God commands, we must obey.
2. Where there is no command, God gives us freedom (and responsibility) to choose.
3. Where there is no command, God gives us wisdom to choose.
4. When we have chosen what is moral and wise, we must trust the sovereign God to work all the details together for good.

Freedom and Responsibility

When Paul talked to unmarried believers who were considering marriage, he was discussing non-commanded decisions. That is, there was no Bible text directing them to marry; nor was there a passage forbidding marriage.[5] And he had no command from the Lord to pass along with apostolic authority that applied to all of them. This was a choice that each of them were free to make, for which they were each responsible.

There is no clearer declaration of this fact in the New Testament than Paul's instructions to widows in the final words of the chapter: "A wife is bound as long as her husband is living. But if her husband dies, she is free to marry anyone she wishes (only someone in the Lord)" (1 Corinthians 7:39).

Just as God had told Adam that he could "freely eat fruit from every tree of the orchard" (Genesis 2:16), so Paul told the Christian widow that "she is free to marry anyone she wishes." Adam was free to eat whatever fruit he liked; the widow was free to marry whatever man she found suitable.

Similarly, in the previous paragraph (7:36-38), Paul instructed a man who was trying to decide if he should marry his fiancée, given the severe difficulties of "the present crisis" (7:26):

> If anyone thinks he is acting inappropriately toward his virgin...*he should do what he wishes;* he does not sin. Let them marry. But the man who is firm in his commitment, and is under no necessity but has control over his will, and *has decided in his own mind* to keep his own virgin, does well.

There were two possible choices: go through with a proposed marriage or not. There were pros and cons for each option, and both choices were acceptable to God. The decision was in the hands of the responsible person.

Moral Limits

But of course the freedom of choice in these matters is not unlimited. And when we describe marital decisions as "non-commanded," we are not claiming that the Bible has *nothing* to say about them. For while these choices are not prescribed by God's moral will, they are regulated by it.

We see moral parameters in Paul's instruction to widows (7:39). This verse begins and ends with two commands that are part of God's moral will. The first is that the marriage covenant is to be a lifelong commitment: "A wife is bound as long as her husband is living." The second command concerns the spiritual status of any man who might become a future spouse: "only someone in the Lord." So these directives fall under the first principle of decision making: "Where God commands, we must obey." A Christian wife is to remain married; but if her husband dies and she chooses to remarry, she must find a husband who is also a believer.

BIBLICAL VIEW OF FREEDOM WITHIN GOD'S MORAL WILL

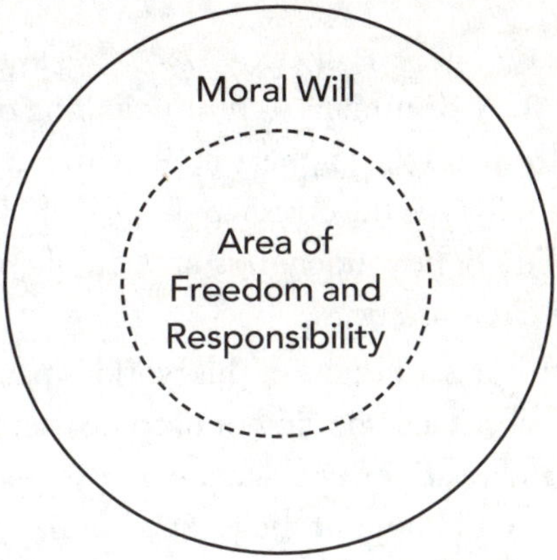

All single men who are not believers are outside the circle of God's moral will—not part of the acceptable pool of marriage prospects. Unmarried Christian men are within the circle, and the choice among them lies within the area of freedom.

Where the King has spoken clearly, disciples are called to obey. As Paul said in this very chapter, "keeping God's commandments is what counts" (7:19). In 1 Corinthians 7:39, the boundary marking off those candidates that are permitted from those that are not is clear and should be taken seriously.[6]

But the application of the principle, "Where God commands, we must obey," extends beyond the prohibition against marrying an unbeliever. As single believers cultivate relationships with members of the opposite sex—whether in casual dating or serious courtship—they must conduct themselves righteously. Christian men and women need to commit to guarding the moral purity not only of their own hearts but of those of their brothers and sisters in Christ.[7]

Wisdom for Decision Making

Unlike me, Paul was not neutral about the marital choices his unmarried readers made. He really wanted as many of them as possible to remain single. Since that option ran counter to cultural expectations, to say nothing of the desires of most single people, he submitted three reasons for choosing celibacy over marriage (7:25-35):

- Because of the "present distress" (7:25-28 ESV). It seems likely that the Corinthians were anticipating or experiencing some form of social upheaval, perhaps famine or political turmoil. Maybe the crisis would prove to be temporary, but it would not be prudent to start a family under such precarious circumstances.
- Because "the present shape of this world is passing away" (7:29-31). Christians should not become overly invested in resources and relationships that are only temporary. Single Christians should not put their hopes for happiness and security in marriage but in the blessings of the age to come.
- Because it is better to be "free from [the] anxieties" of marriage and to give "undivided devotion to the Lord" (7:32-35 ESV). Paul was recruiting special forces who would seize the freedom of their single state to serve the King with undistracted devotion.

Paul was a celibate man who appreciated the benefits of his single state. His challenge for others to join his ranks was based on pastoral concern not only for their service to the Lord but for their personal well-being (7:35). In his personal judgment, they would be "happier" if, under the present circumstances, they chose to remain single (7:40).

But Paul was also a realist, and he knew there were strong reasons for choosing marriage. One in particular—the desire for sexual communion with a spouse—is potent because it is built into one's nature. Paul himself had been gifted with the ability to serve God as a single person without being unduly distracted by sexual impulses. But he knew that wasn't necessarily the case for everyone else. So he conceded that "it is better to marry than to burn with sexual desire" (7:7-9).

Paul's approach demonstrates the Way of Wisdom. He was offering counsel on a decision where the choices were not between right and wrong but good and better (7:8-9,26,38). He is very clear that either choice is acceptable to God (7:28,36-38), and that the decision maker must use wisdom to weigh the pros and cons of each option. His reference to "the present crisis" indicates that one option might be preferable under one set of circumstances, while the alternative might be better if the situation were to change. At all times, wisdom gives the highest priority to the believer's devotion to God.

Factoring in God's Sovereign Will

Even as he dispenses counsel to Corinthian believers regarding their marital choices, Paul is aware—and makes a point to remind his readers—that another factor is at play: the sovereign will of God. At the centerpiece of his discourse (7:17-24), he underscores the truth set out in the opening words of verse 17 (HCSB): "each one must live his life in the situation the Lord assigned when God called him."[8] That is, all of our external circumstances (ethnic, social, marital) come to us as an assignment from God.

Why are you single? Because that is your sovereignly determined status. What do you do with that information? Paul invites three responses.

1. Accept your assignment.

This is where Paul's guideline to "remain as you are" comes into play. His initial challenge to the Corinthian believers was to resist the worldly impulse to immediately try to change their circumstances. This is a call, first of all, to trust in God's providential goodness and to find contentment in the provisions of his grace. This is well expressed by Eugene Peterson's paraphrase of 1 Corinthians 7:17 (MSG): "And don't be wishing you were someplace else or with someone else. Where you are right now is God's place for you. Live and obey and love and believe right there. God, not your marital status, defines your life."

2. Embrace your assignment.

The directive "remain as you are" (7:26) is not simply a call to passive resignation. In verse 17, the parallel verb is the command "to walk"

(NASB)—one of Paul's favorite words for purposeful involvement. The NIV conveys this sense of dynamic engagement: "Each person should *live as a believer* in whatever situation the Lord has assigned to them." This refers to an active participation with God in the current circumstances of my life—to make the most of the opportunities that exist in my present situation to advance his kingdom.

3. Explore opportunities for improvement.

God's sovereign will is not static. When Paul counseled "remain as you are," he was not slamming the door on change. This fact is clear from his parenthetical comment to slaves—"But *if indeed you are able* to be free, make the most of the opportunity" (7:21). Of all people, slaves had the fewest opportunities for decision making. But sometimes a master would offer freedom, and Paul didn't want his essential counsel to block an indentured believer from accepting a legitimate release from slavery.

Similarly, single people may have the opportunity to marry. Change is possible—and permissible—though in this case, the movement is from freedom to servitude.[9]

But what does "if you are able" mean to single adults in today's world? How much initiative is appropriate? The Corinthian slave was at the mercy of his master; he was powerless to extract his own freedom. Are you likewise obliged to passively wait until God sovereignly drops a suitable mate in your lap?

No. The range of options available to the modern-day single adult is much broader than that of the first-century slave. You not only have the opportunity to seek out and court a potential spouse, but your active participation in the process may be all the more necessary given the absence of mate selection by parents or matchmakers. Sometimes an unmarried person meets their future spouse through a magical, serendipitous encounter. But more marriages come about as a result of deliberate actions by those who eventually wed.

In his book *The Marriage Builder,* Larry Crabb strikes the biblical balance when he advises: *Pray for your desires; work for your goals.* Here he makes an important distinction between desires and goals. A *goal,* in this instance, is an objective that is under my control. I can attain it through diligent effort. A *desire*, on the other hand, is something I want but cannot obtain on my own—I need the cooperation of another person(s). If I hope to get married, I can make it my *goal* to become a mature Christian who acts for the welfare of others. No one can keep me from doing that, and such growth and commitment may open the door to a significant relationship with marriage potential. My *desire* to find an available mate who is on a similar trajectory is beyond my control. Since that outcome is ultimately governed by God's sovereign will, that is a legitimate subject for prayer (see Philippians 4:6). As Crabb says, "The proper response to a desire, then, is *prayer.* To a goal, the appropriate response is a set of *responsible actions.*"[10]

This approach applies the principles of the Way of Wisdom. In noncommanded decisions, the believer is free and responsible to make choices within the moral will of God as directed by wisdom. In the interplay between your responsibility and God's sovereign will, you are free to make plans and carry out strategies. (In part 4, "Looking for a Mate," I have identified some specific elements you might want to include in your plan.)

But you must subject your plans to God's sovereign will and trust him to bring about his purposes, which are also for your good (Romans 8:28; James 4:13-16). One way to express this submission is through prayer (Romans 1:10).[11]

The Rest of the Story

The third response to God's sovereign will, "Explore opportunities for improvement," raises the question whether marriage is an *improvement* for someone who is single. If 1 Corinthians 7 provided the only window into Paul's thinking on the subject, we might conclude that his answer is no. In this treatise, Paul provides only one substantial reason for some to choose marriage—it is the only sanctioned state for engaging in sexual intercourse.

Well, this is not the only place where Paul expresses his perspectives on marriage and, as you might suppose, there is more to it than we have seen so far. In fact, God's design for marriage encompasses far more than most people know—or even imagine.

An improvement over singleness? Keep reading.

Don't Forget...

- Marital choices are non-commanded decisions. Single Christians have the freedom and responsibility to make their own decisions within the moral will of God.
- For Christians who choose to marry, the moral will of God limits the pool of acceptable candidates to fellow believers in Christ.
- Both singleness and marriage have pros and cons. These should be identified and evaluated on the basis of wisdom.
- As you weigh your options, consider which one will most enhance your devotion and service to the Lord.
- Since your marital status at any given time is established by the sovereign will of God, you should accept your present status as an assignment from God and maximize the advantages it provides to advance his kingdom. But if you are single, you are free to explore opportunities for marriage that may open up by God's sovereign will.
- As you devise plans to pursue your hopes, pray for your desires and work for your goals.

To access the endnotes and for questions for reflection and group discussion go to:

www.TheMarriageDecision.com

PART 3

God's Design for Marriage

MODERN MYTH 3

The key to a successful marriage is to find and marry one's soul mate.

INTRODUCTION TO PART 3

God's Design for Marriage

Every April, one of the rites of spring that captures the attention of gridiron fans is the Player Selection Meeting of the National Football League (a.k.a. the NFL draft). Over a two-day span, officials of the thirty-two NFL teams select new players from the ranks of college upperclassmen to join their rosters. Each team devotes countless hours of research, millions of dollars, and the energies of the most-talented scouts and executives in football to make the personnel choices the fortunes of each team will ride on in the years to come.

The decisions involved in player selection are complex. The basic objective of each team is to identify and draft the most-talented players to fill specific positions. A team's needs are based on the style of play determined by the philosophy of the head coach and the strengths of the veterans already on the roster. The qualifications that define the ideal player for each position are very exacting. The trick is to find a match between the profile for each position and the best available candidate—before another team grabs your preferred choice.

"OK, I see where you're going with this," you say to me. "You're making the point that one's choice of a spouse is at least as important as the selection of a football player. So I should give a lot of consideration to the kind of person who would be a good match for me and carefully evaluate potential mates by a thoughtfully crafted set of criteria."

Very good!

But no, that's not my point. Not yet.

To get to my point we must create an imaginary scenario. Suppose you were offered a job to become director of player personnel for a professional sports team. Let's assume that you are athletically inclined and avidly interested in sports, so this would be a dream job. For the record, you are also energetic and perceptive. Your first assignment would be to oversee the team of scouts and coaches preparing for the upcoming player draft. Even though the task appears daunting, the position is just too good to pass up. Just as you are about to sign on the dotted line, you read one last but extremely important detail in your contract.

The sport in question is *cricket.*

Since I'm the one making up this fantasy, you don't get to tear up the contract. Instead, you're intrigued. *Why*, you wonder, *would anyone want to recruit me to this position?* And the very first thing you say to the general manager who has offered you this job is, "I don't know anything about cricket.[1] Why, I wouldn't know a googly from a grubber."

"I know," the general manager says. "We're looking for someone with your energy and perceptiveness, but who will bring the fresh perspective of a novice to the game."

And now we are closing in on my point. If you were hired to draft players for a sport you know nothing about, what is the first thing you would do? Surely you would set about to learn everything you could about that sport. You might go so far as to read the forty-two rules in *The Laws of Cricket.* Only then would you begin to have a clue about what sort of players you should be looking for.

You don't evaluate the players until you understand the game.

Nancy is a school teacher, but she has some homework of her own to complete.

We met Nancy in the introduction to part 2: "God's Design for Singleness." As we reflected on her circumstances as an unmarried woman, we identified the three stages single persons typically navigate en route to marriage:

- Stage 1: Not ready
- Stage 2: Available—but no specific prospects
- Stage 3: Courtship with a live candidate

Nancy is in Stage 2. She is in the market for a husband and is ready to put together a plan to find one—or, perhaps, to get herself found by one. And she has a pretty good idea of what she's looking for. She's grown past her childhood fantasies of the handsome prince who gallops in to rescue her on his white stallion (well, mostly). What she really wants is a soul mate—a complementary companion who will mesh with her personality, values, and aspirations; someone who will be her best friend, and lover, for life. Also, he needs to be a Christian.

She used to think that God would pick out her husband and bring him to her. But a book she has been reading has convinced her that that idea is a myth. So she has embraced her God-given freedom and responsibility and is taking initiative to look for a mate. She is praying that God will give her success in her quest and asking for wisdom to make moral and prudent choices.

In her enthusiasm over the prospect of actually doing something to get off dead center, she is inclined to forge ahead in designing a plan. But her study of 1 Corinthians 7 inserted an intermediate step in the process. She found herself challenged by the apostle Paul to carefully evaluate the advantages and challenges of singleness and marriage before settling on a direction. What remains from that project is an assessment of marriage. She thinks she had a pretty good idea of what marriage is about, but she has realized that the subject is serious enough to make sure she isn't overlooking something important. So she has decided to complete the assignment.

After all, *you don't evaluate the players until you understand the game.*

What Nancy doesn't realize is that while she has a good enough understanding of the "game" of marriage to be a fan and a spectator, she isn't anywhere near ready to engage in candidate evaluation—to say nothing of player selection. For instance, she doesn't know that there are currently *three different versions* of the game being played in our culture. Before she can even begin to think about qualifications for a mate, she will need to choose which model of marriage she intends to pursue. The last thing she needs is a spouse who is playing a whole different game with a different set of rules.

And that's just for starters.

To get her bearings, Nancy needs to confer with the Person who invented the game in the first place. Get back to original design.

It's time to consult the Owner's Manual.

The Story of Marriage

The Bible, of course, isn't organized like *The Laws of Cricket.* There may be forty-two "rules of marriage," but you won't find them in a sequential list. "God's Design for Marriage" unfolds in a kind of story—a historical chronicle in which adaptations are made to the original prototype.

Jesus referred to that story in a narrative we have already encountered (chapter 3). Religious opponents tried to suck him into a raging debate about what constituted legitimate grounds for divorce. "Is it lawful to divorce a wife for any cause?" they asked (Matthew 19:3). They expected that any answer he gave would alienate a sizable portion of a divided public. But Jesus didn't rise to the bait. He rebuked them for asking the wrong question, for focusing in the wrong direction.

> "Have you not read that from the beginning the Creator 'made them male and female,' and said, 'For this reason a man will leave his father and mother and will be united with his wife, and the two will become one flesh'? So they are no longer two, but one flesh. Therefore what God has joined together, let no one separate." They said to him, "Why then did Moses command us to give 'a certificate of dismissal' and to divorce her?" Jesus said to them, "Moses permitted you to divorce your wives because of your hard hearts, but from the beginning it was not this way. Now I say to you that whoever divorces his wife, except for immorality, and marries another commits adultery" (Matthew 19:4-9).

Jesus didn't debate. Speaking with Messianic authority, he corrected the myths of his day and explained the divine intent behind the statements of Scripture. In this brief exchange, he underscored important elements in the Story of Marriage.

- Marriage was ordained by God; it is not a human invention.
- The original design for marriage is grounded in the created nature of humankind as male and female.
- Marriage was intended to unite a husband and wife in a permanent and unbreakable bond.
- Along the way, something terrible happened. Spouses with "hard hearts" invoked divorce to sever what God had joined together.
- Nevertheless, God's original intent for marriage is still valid—even in a fallen world.

Jesus's use of the Story of Marriage to straighten out the thinking of his audience indicates that understanding the big picture is fundamental to grasping God's design. Nancy won't learn everything she needs to know by studying Genesis 2 or Ephesians 5. She needs to see how it all began, what went wrong, what God is doing about it, and how it's all going to turn out.

The whole Story of Marriage that Jesus invoked runs through the entire Bible—literally from beginning to end. It develops through four acts that anyone can follow:

THE STORY OF MARRIAGE

Act 1: God made it.

Act 2: We broke it.

Act 3: Jesus remade it.

Act 4: All Christians will experience it.

So here's what we're going to do with Nancy:

1. We're going to tell the story.
2. We're going to identify the elements of God's design for marriage[2] and compare them to the other "games" in town.
3. As she considers whether she wants to marry, she can adopt deliberate reasons for her choices.
4. If she is inclined toward matrimony, she can choose which version of marriage she wants to pursue.
5. Once she fully understands the game, she can identify the qualities of the player she would like to draft.
6. Then she can develop a plan for recruitment.

You are cordially invited to tag along.

Chapter 5

Marriage: God Made It

"What's with all the *beaming*?"

From his perch next to the groom, Jay surveyed the other members of the troupe that had been assembled to enact this ritual drama. Everybody was beaming. The bridesmaids were beaming, the pastor was beaming, the groom was beaming, the groomsmen were glowing in a masculine sort of way, and the bride—well, she was off-the-chart radiant. Everybody was emitting mega-lumens of joy—except, of course, the father of the bride, who was a basket case and just trying to hold it together.

Beaming, Jay reflected, is something people do only at weddings.

Even he was probably reflecting the joy he felt for his best friend, Art, who was about to commit himself to a lifelong union with the love of his life, Becky. The only shadow cast over Jay's heart was the dashed expectation that he would beat Art to the altar.

Jay gave himself an imaginary smack in the back of the head. *Don't go there now, buddy. This isn't about you.*

He was glad Art and Becky had opted for a traditional ceremony. The script contained everything that needed to be said and done to institute a marriage, to launch a new family. And all the participants knew the drill. Also, it didn't last long, which was a virtue to a best man whose mind tended to wander.

The return of Jay's focus to the matter at hand coincided with the conclusion of the pastor's homily. Now it was Art's turn, and Jay's attention was absolute.

> I, Arthur, take you, Rebecca, to be my lawfully wedded wife; to have and to hold, from this day forward, for better, for worse, for richer, for poorer, in sickness or in health, to love and to cherish till death do us part. And hereto I pledge you my faithfulness.

What an astounding pledge. Here were two people, in love at the moment, promising to cherish and care for each other for the rest of their lives. They look off into an unknown future and agree to be partners in life for maybe twice as long as they have lived singly. Could such promises possibly be kept?

Jay smiled. He knew the answer. One week from tonight, many from this same cast of characters would reassemble to celebrate the fiftieth anniversary of his grandparents, Papa and Nana Chambers. He couldn't help but wonder what they were thinking as they listened, for the hundredth time, to vows of marital faithfulness.

"This is a profound mystery," the pastor had said, quoting the Bible. Well, even apostles were permitted a few understatements. Marriage is indeed a remarkable institution, and one Jay had entertained high hopes for—until recently. Who knows? Maybe he would again someday.

"What token do you give as the public symbol..."

Token? Symbol?

Rings!

Jay was jerked back to his assignment. Now, which pocket...?

* * * * * * * *

Through the millennia there have been a lot of weddings. In every culture, men and women get paired up somehow and become mates. With rare exceptions, marriages are initiated by ceremonies (with varying degrees of formality) where the bride and groom stand before representatives of their community and make vows of lifelong fidelity. The details of the various traditions differ, but the ingredients are remarkably similar. This has gone on for generation after generation, in family after family.

The universality of this human convention is striking. Indeed, we commonly refer to this arrangement as the *institution* of marriage. And we know how it was instituted. According to the Bible, the history of civilization began with the first wedding.[1] Looking back, the degree of continuity between the original and the variations throughout human history is remarkable.

When we wonder how to account for this consistency, the biblical record explains that it is due to two things: the way human beings were formed in the first place and the relational patterns established by the Creator for our well-being.

Purpose—What Marriage Is For

Act 1 of the Story of Marriage is recorded in Genesis 1–2[2] and unfolds through four scenes:

1. the *mission* of the first couple (1:26-28)
2. the *creation* of the first couple (2:7,18-22a)
3. the *"wedding"* of the first couple (2:22b-25)
4. the *pattern* established by the first couple (2:24)

Through these four scenes, the narrator addresses our questions about marriage. Among other things, we learn the unique *identity* of the first couple, the *role* God assigned to them, the *mission* they were to undertake, and the *functions* of marriage through which their mission was to be carried out. As these features of the story are narrated, God's original design for marriage emerges.

Scene 1: The Mission of the First Couple (Genesis 1:26-28)

The first human couple is introduced to us (and to the world) as the culmination of God's creative work on the sixth day.

> Then God said, "Let us make humankind in our image, after our likeness, so they may rule over the fish of the sea and the birds of the air, over the cattle, and over all the earth, and over all the creatures that move on the earth."

> God created humankind in his own image,
> in the image of God he created them,
> male and female he created them.
>
> God blessed them and said to them, "Be fruitful and multiply! Fill the earth and subdue it! Rule over the fish of the sea and the birds of the air and every creature that moves on the ground" (Genesis 1:26-28).

The biblical narrator first describes the creation of human beings in a succinct summary. In these introductory statements, three things stand out about the first people: who they are (their identity), their place in the created order (their role), and what they are to do (their mission).

Who are they? They are creatures "in the image and likeness of God."[3] While human beings are similar in many ways to the other created beings, we are different in at least two ways. First, in our essential identity as image-bearers, we resemble or correspond to the Creator in unique ways. Like him, we have a spiritual nature (Genesis 9:6; Colossians 3:10; James 3:9), personality (intellect, emotion, will), and moral sensitivities revealed in a conscience. Because these attributes are part of our *essence*, human beings have the capacity to interact with God in a person-to-person relationship. That's who we are.

What is their role? A second difference between humans and lower life-forms is that the image-bearers act on God's behalf to rule over all the other creatures. This is one aspect of the mandate to "multiply... subdue...and rule over" the earth. With authority delegated from the sovereign King, the image-bearers function as vice-regents (junior rulers). Just as the Creator had brought order to planet earth, colonizing it with creatures who reflect his likeness, so his representatives were to subdue and rule the earth, imposing order on their world and populating it with offspring in their image (Genesis 5:3).[4]

What are they to do? The other thing we learn from this opening scene is the *mission* of the original image-bearers. Adam and Eve (and their offspring) were to serve God by advancing his rule over the earth.[5]

So in one brief paragraph, three key characteristics of God's design for humanity are identified:

- Their identity: Adam and Eve were *image-bearers* who reflected the nature of their Creator.
- Their role: Adam and Eve were to rule over the earth as God's representative *vice-regents*.
- Their mission: Adam and Eve were to serve God by *advancing his rule* over the earth.

Before we move on to the next segment, we must take note of one additional detail in the summary passage: "male and female he created them." There are two genders, and both are required to adequately represent the nature of God and to carry out the assigned mission. The establishment and nature of the male-female partnership is chronicled in the next two scenes.

Scene 2: The Creation of the First Couple (Genesis 2:7,18-22a)

I wish I could somehow recreate for you the experience of encountering the opening chapters of the Bible for the first time. I wish you could revert to a time of childlike innocence where you ask God, "Where did we all come from? How did it all begin?" And he would hand you Genesis 1–2 and say, "Here, read this." Or maybe he would give you a DVD and let you watch it. I think you might be astonished by the story. For one thing, you would be surprised to learn that the first humans were not created simultaneously nor in the same way.

> The LORD God formed the man from the soil of the ground and breathed into his nostrils the breath of life, and the man became a living being...
>
> The LORD God took the man and placed him in the orchard in Eden to care for and maintain it. Then the LORD God commanded the man, "You may freely eat fruit from every tree of the orchard, but you must not eat from the tree of the knowledge of good and evil, for when you eat from it you will surely die" (Genesis 2:7,15-17).

The man came into being as God formed his body from the earth and animated him with "the breath of life."[6] Then the Lord God placed the man in the Garden of Eden "to care for and maintain it."[7] With this assignment came one limitation: "you must not eat from the tree of the knowledge of good and evil, for when you eat from it you will surely die" (2:17). In this way, the man's moral nature (part of the divine image) was engaged and put to the test.

So far so good. The observer of the creation account has been cruising along for forty-eight verses and the construction project has proceeded according to plan, on schedule, within budget. And it's all been good, good, good...very good. But now there's a problem. It was not unforeseen by the Owner-Contractor, but it is shocking to the viewer.

> The LORD God said, "It is not good for the man to be alone" (2:18).

Right here we need to hit the pause button. In a perfect world, what could possibly be "not good"? What's wrong with a man-by-himself?

At one level, nothing; the man was not defective. But there was something about him that was *incomplete*. That is a point worth noting: Adam, as he was in himself, was incomplete *by design*. Human beings were not created to be solitary creatures. We have a built-in capacity and need for relationship. Adam needed help.

So what is God going to do about it? Hit rewind and then hit play.

> The LORD God said, "It is not good for the man to be alone. I will make a companion for him who corresponds to him" (2:18).

Pause again. Adam needs a companion, so God is going to make one for him. How is he going to proceed? This is not a complicated problem. He's already done this once. Just scoop up another handful of dirt, breathe into it, and voilà! There's enough work in Eden for two men, and Adam will have a pal. Mission accomplished!

But Adam didn't need a clone; he needed a companion. Not someone essentially identical to him but someone corresponding to him—his "opposite" in a complementary way.[8]

> So the LORD God caused the man to fall into a deep sleep, and while he was asleep, he took part of the man's side and closed up the place with flesh. Then the LORD God made a woman from the part he had taken out of the man, and he brought her to the man (2:21-22).

Rather than duplicating the process by which he created the man from the dust of the ground, God used a dramatically different approach—he formed the woman *from* the man's side.[9] Therefore, she corresponded to him precisely.

Scene 3: The "Wedding" of the First Couple (Genesis 2:22b-25)

Weddings can be complicated affairs. By contrast, the first one was pretty simple. There was no gown, no tux, no rings—just the bare essentials. But there were lots of flowers.

First, the bride was created *from* the man. Then she was presented *to* the man. (The Creator in this instance takes his place as "the father of the bride.")[10]

> Then the LORD God made a woman from the part he had taken out of the man, and he brought her to the man. Then the man said,
>
> "This one at last is bone of my bones
> and flesh of my flesh;
> this one will be called 'woman,'
> for she was taken out of man."
>
> (Genesis 2:22-23)

Adam's reaction to this wonder of a creation was an "outburst of love poetry."[11] (He was beaming, no doubt.) Nonpoetic paraphrase: "Wow! She's just like me—only different!" God had provided what Adam had been searching for—a companion perfectly suited to him. As she stands next to him, we see two persons who share equally in their essence as image-bearers. It was long ago observed, and oft repeated, that woman was taken not from man's head to be ruler over him, nor from man's foot to be his servant, but from his side to be his companion.[12]

The Functions of Marriage

What do scenes 2 and 3 reveal about marriage? With the creation of Eve and the explanation of why she was added to the mix, we get insight into the nature of marriage. Specifically, when we recognize the kind of help that Adam needed and Eve provided, we can identify the *functions* of marriage.

Relational togetherness is clearly one provision. Because of her company with him, not only would neither of them be solitary, neither of them would be lonely.

But there's one other way the woman's help was needed. The assignment to "be fruitful and multiply, to fill the earth and subdue it" was not a one-man job. For starters, the woman was necessary for the task of reproduction. And, by extension, she was to assist Adam in carrying out all of his God-given responsibilities, of which procreation was only one. Notice that God's determination to "make a corresponding companion" immediately follows (1) his assignment to Adam to tend the Garden of Eden, and (2) his commandment forbidding Adam to eat from the tree of the knowledge of good and evil (Genesis 2:15-18). Adam needed more than company. He needed help in fulfilling his responsibilities and keeping God's commandments.[13]

And so there are *two functions* for marriage: (1) loving companionship and (2) working partnership. Please take note: this is a major point of this book. The first couple was given a *relationship* to cultivate and a *work* to share, which included procreation. In the succinct terminology of Dan Allender and Tremper Longman III, they were to be *intimate allies*.[14]

(Procreation is such an essential component of the original design of marriage that a strong case can be made for recognizing reproduction as a third function—on a par with relational companionship and working partnership. In this book, I classify procreation under the broader category of a couple's shared work. But I do not want to minimize its importance in our understanding of what marriage is about.

By God's design, most husbands and wives become fathers and mothers. Children are a gift from the Lord [Psalm 127:3], and parents are to work together to raise up "godly offspring" [Malachi 2:15 NIV].)

To sum up: from the first three scenes, we are able to see that God's intent for marriage is strongly related to his overarching plan for human beings. In God's original design, marriage was a provision given to men and women to help them accomplish their shared *mission* to serve God by advancing his rule on the earth. This purpose was accomplished as the husband and wife fulfilled the marital *functions* of working partnership and loving companionship.

In our clarification of this design, we must not overlook the significance of the words "to serve God." In the following paragraphs, we will emphasize that the bond between a husband and wife is to be the strongest human allegiance. *But that relationship was never intended to be ultimate.* Before they were spouses, the man and woman were image-bearing creatures.[15] Their relationship to the Creator was to take precedence over any responsibility they might have to each other. Their shared assignment required recognition of the supreme authority of the King.[16]

Scene 4: The Pattern Established by the First Couple (Genesis 2:24)

The fourth scene is different from the previous three. In it, the Playwright of the Story of Marriage walks onto the stage and utters a single line. Rather than leaving the audience to guess at the implications of the story line, he spells out the moral in no uncertain terms.

> Therefore a man leaves his father and his mother and cleaves to his wife, and they become one flesh (Genesis 2:24 RSV).[17]

There can be only one first couple, only one first wedding. By the time Genesis was written, grooms and brides were not directly created by God. But God wanted them (and us) to understand an essential connection between the first marriage and all that followed it. And so he tells us that the first marriage provided a pattern for all others: "Therefore a man leaves..." or "That is why a man leaves..."[18]

And here is the main idea: *If a man and a woman are going to become lifelong working partners and loving companions, they must forge the strongest possible bond of commitment between them from the very beginning of the marriage.*

Pattern—What Marriage Is

This bond consists of two elements: (1) "a man leaves his father and his mother and cleaves to his wife," and (2) "they become one flesh."[19]

Leave and *cleave* are two very strong verbs. *Leaving* often has the sense of "forsaking" or "abandoning." This is what the husband is told to do with regard to his parents.[20] In this way, the loyalty of marriage is elevated above all other commitments, under God.

To "cleave" or "hold fast" (ESV) is the positive complement to "leave." The word connotes a very strong bond, much like glue.[21] In this decisive commitment, husband and wife together establish a new family unit that takes precedence over all others.

Taken together, "leaving and cleaving" comprise the *public commitment* to faithfulness that historically has been the function of the wedding. In the progressive revelation of the Old Testament, this commitment came to be defined in terms of a covenant[22] (Proverbs 2:16-17;[23] Ezekiel 16:8; Malachi 2:14-16). A covenant is the most binding of human agreements—stronger in its intent than a contract. The marriage covenant provided a guarantee of lifelong loyalty that offered security to both parties in the relationship because of the extreme level of commitment promised.

At the moment the marital pledge is made, the marriage is established.[24] But while the groom and bride, by virtue of their public vows, are legally *bound*, they are not yet physically and emotionally *bonded*.[25] For the pattern to be completed, the "leaving and cleaving" must lead to becoming "one flesh." This clearly points to the sexual union in which the couple literally and physically experiences a one-flesh connection.[26] But it is equally clear that the sexual aspect is a sign and expression of a union that joins husband and wife at every level. More than a union of two bodies, "one flesh" describes the joining of two lives.[27] So the NET Bible translates the statement: "That is why a man leaves his father and mother and unites with his wife, and they become a new family."[28]

So while "leaving and cleaving" speak of the *public covenant* in which faithfulness is promised, "becoming one flesh" refers to the *private consummation* in which faithfulness is kept and expanded into a fully shared life. These two aspects together constitute the essence of marriage.

God's Pattern For Marriage

"Leave and cleave"	→	"Become one flesh"
Wedding	→	Honeymoon and marriage
Public covenant	→	Private consummation
Faithfulness promised	→	Faithfulness kept
Legally bound	→	Physically, emotionally bonded

In the God-given pattern, a marriage is begun with a decisive commitment and sustained by unified, daily faithfulness to the covenant. Not only are both components important, but the sequence is significant. The couple does not "become one flesh" and *then* leave father and mother. First there is a wedding, and then the couple live together as husband and wife. That's how we've been doing it for thousands of years because that's how it was designed from the beginning.

One more aspect to the pattern was established in the marriage of the first couple. Just as God brought the first husband and wife together and rejoined them into a dynamic unity, so he similarly unites every groom and bride who pledge loyalty to each other in marriage. Jesus said, "What God has joined together, let no one separate" (Matthew 19:6).[29] So when a man and woman commit themselves to be faithful to the covenant of marriage, God is a partner in the creation of their union. And every wedding is a sacred event.[30]

Based on the Story of Marriage narrated in Genesis 1–2, John Stott supplies this biblical definition of marriage: "Marriage is an exclusive heterosexual covenant between one man and one woman, ordained and sealed by God, preceded by a public leaving of parents, consummated in sexual union, issuing in a permanent mutually supportive partnership, and normally crowned by the gift of children."[31]

That's how it started out.

••••••••

If Adam and Eve had stuck with the divinely established pattern in obedient fulfillment of God's original purpose for marriage, the Story of Marriage might have consisted of one act. (And this book would not have been necessary.) But they didn't, and we don't. It's not all bad news. But to get to the good news, we have to confront some pretty harsh reality. Act 2 is not for the squeamish.

Be brave. You can do it. Just read the next chapter.

••••••••

Don't Forget...

- God's *pattern* for marriage includes two elements: a public covenant in which faithfulness is promised ("leaving and cleaving"), and private consummation in which faithfulness is kept and expanded into a fully shared life ("becoming one flesh").
- The original *purpose* of marriage was to enable men and women to accomplish their shared *mission* to serve God by advancing his rule on the earth.
- The purpose of marriage is accomplished as the husband and wife fulfill the two primary *functions* of working partnership and loving companionship.

- In a godly marriage, each spouse's relationship to the other is secondary to and dependent upon their *higher allegiance* to the sovereign Creator.

To access the endnotes and for questions for reflection and group discussion go to:

www.TheMarriageDecision.com

CHAPTER 6

Marriage: We Broke It

Jay sipped sparkling cider from a plastic champagne glass as he watched his grandparents slow dance in the center of the banquet room. Mr. and Mrs. Harold Chambers had been married for fifty years, and this was their grand celebration. Remarkably well-preserved, Papa and Nana provided solid evidence for the hypothesis that "seventy is the new sixty." What struck Jay is how comfortable they seemed to be in each other's arms.

Equally striking was the absence of other couples that one might have expected to see on the dance floor, such as his own parents. His mother, Linda, was dutifully carrying out her responsibilities as anniversary hostess for her parents, but her solo status was made all the more conspicuous by the occasion. Jay's dad, Bill, had been out of the picture since their divorce when Jay was eight. Bill had remarried, and the focus of his fatherly attention had shifted away from Jay and his sister to stepchildren acquired in the new deal. Linda had done her best to fulfill both parental roles as a single mom, and Jay appreciated the effort—just as he admired the way she was honoring the long-term fidelity of her parents.

The other couple missing from the dance was Jay and Cindy. He had expected that they would attend the party together when they received the invitation three months previous. But Cindy exercised her option and moved out the weekend his baseball team was away for the three-game series with Syracuse. He never saw it coming. Other couples they knew had broken up, but in most of those cases, it was the guy who bailed. But, according to her note, Cindy had gotten a better offer...

Jay's eyes moved from the swaying couple celebrating a half-century of marriage to the solitary form of his mother at the refreshment table. It was largely to avoid her fate that he had invited Cindy to move in with him. It had made sense at the time. Try it out. No strings. Make sure we're compatible. And above all, let's avoid putting our kids through the wrenching losses we experienced as children. So, mission accomplished. No kids were damaged—except for the one attending his grandparents' anniversary party with a fractured heart still wounded by the desertion of his father. Nobody had told him breaking up would hurt like, well, a divorce.

Jay was startled by a sudden shift in the volume and tempo of the music and the rhythmic flashing of strobe lights. His attention was yanked back to the dance floor by the astounding gyrations of two septuagenarians rocking out to the Beach Boys' "Surfin' USA." There, before his eyes, was a living, dancing portrayal of what he hoped for in a marriage. His prospects, at that moment, seemed remote.

How had it gotten to be so hard?

Act 2: We Broke It

For the record, I know a lot of people who have happy marriages. I even know quite a few whose marriages turned out to be better than they had dreamed—though almost always for different reasons than they expected. I am in that happy camp. Being married to Louise has been a great blessing in my life.

But I have also witnessed the twisted wreckage that resulted from the collision of high hopes and hidden, sabotaging realities. Divorce has ravaged the lives of some of my dearest friends and has wreaked its havoc in my own extended family. As I survey the devastation of wounded lives, I see real faces in my mind's eye. And I write these words through tears of grief and rage. The pain is not theoretical; the loss is not just something that happens to other people. And my hatred of it, which I share with Almighty God (Malachi 2:16), is one of the driving forces behind the publication of this book.

I wish there was something I could write (and you could read) that would guarantee a happy marital outcome for everyone. Alas, we have the Bible, and people still botch things. One huge reason for that is the upheaval that took place in Act 2 of the human drama. The original couple made choices that knocked everything out of kilter—including us. So now the individuals who make marital choices are impaired, and the surrounding forces that most influence our thinking are misguided and, therefore, deceptive.

The mess we're in is big.

I don't like Act 2 and I'm tempted to sidestep it. But denial only makes things worse. No, if we're going to make grown-up decisions, we need to be grown up in our willingness to confront what we're up against. Skipping over this part would be like deciding to play tackle football without putting on a helmet or shoulder pads. Ignorance of the impact of sin, and the failure to take countermeasures against it (Genesis 4:7), may be the single greatest cause of marital breakup.

As train wrecks go, this one is a humdinger.

It's Our Parents' Fault

You are probably familiar with the incident involving the diabolical serpent, the gullible woman, the passive male, and the delectable-but-toxic fruit. (If not, you should put this book down and read through Genesis 3). In their disobedience of God's command (Genesis 2:16-17), the first couple violated every component of their assignment.

- Instead of ruling over the creatures, they submitted to one—the serpent.
- Instead of helping her husband, the woman contributed to his downfall.
- Instead of trusting in God's provision, they believed the lie that he was holding out on them.
- Instead of being satisfied with being like God as image-bearers, they became dissatisfied with their position as creatures and lusted for more.

- Instead of serving God through their obedience, they rebelled.

And, as God had promised, they died. Oh, they didn't cease to exist. But the death that they experienced was worse than extinction. The lethal penalty crashed in upon them in successive waves as they were wrenched from the realm of life to the realm of death (Genesis 3:8-24).

Before the Rebellion, the first couple enjoyed unhindered communion with their Creator. The greatest blessing Adam and Eve experienced was not their marriage; it was their fellowship with God. They forfeited this blessing by their rebellion. The worst thing that happened to them was their expulsion from God's presence (Genesis 3:23-24). As exiles, they were cut off from the Source of life. To repeat, *this is the worst thing that could happen to human beings.* No other problem even comes close.

Before the Rebellion, the first couple enjoyed the benefits of working partnership and loving companionship—the marital functions designed by God: Now every aspect of the marriage relationship was corrupted.

- *Companionship*: the intimacy of a one-flesh relationship was immediately fractured by alienation, blame, and shame (3:7-12).
- *Procreation*: childbirth was now attended by pain and sorrow (3:16).
- *Shared vocation*: the domain they were to rule over now rebelled against them, turning meaningful labor into life-sapping toil (3:17-19).

Before the Rebellion, the first couple enjoyed the dignity of participating in a God-ordained mission that gave meaning and significance to their work. They had been vice-regents in charge of everything else. Now they were unemployed, homeless nomads. And their lives were filled with regret and frustration as they put all their efforts into mere survival—a mission doomed to ultimately fail.

As it turns out, these horrific consequences were not limited to Adam and Eve. What they handed off to their offspring was nothing less than cosmic disarray. The upheaval caused by the Rebellion was pervasive, reaching down through the centuries to our own time.

While the effects of the Rebellion were extensive, we are mainly interested in its impact on marriage. As you contemplate marital decisions, two repercussions warrant your careful attention. The first is the corrupting influence of sin in the life of every spouse. The second is the warping of marriage itself from the harmonious partnership of Eden to an imbalanced relationship tainted by the pull of selfish desire.

Up Close and Personal

It was the Creator himself who gave the definitive assessment of sin's impact on married people.

> To the woman he said,
> "I will surely multiply your pain in childbearing;
> in pain you shall bring forth children.
> Your desire shall be for your husband,
> and he shall rule over you."
>
> (Genesis 3:16 ESV)

Scholars debate the precise meaning of this pronouncement.[1] But this much is clear: spousal harmony was replaced by conflict in which the stronger came to domineer the weaker. As commentator Derek Kidner put it: "'To love and to cherish' becomes 'To desire and to dominate.'"[2] And so began the centuries-long soap opera featuring the heavy-handed subjugation of women by men and the manipulative intrigues of scheming wives.[3]

How does this affect you personally? The infection of sin extends to you and any future spouse (Romans 3:23; 5:12; Ephesians 2:1-2). If you marry, the person you marry will be a sinner. And the person he or she marries will be a sinner. That's two sinners in close proximity to each other for long stretches of time. Your spouse will undoubtedly have many fine qualities, as do you. But you will need to pay attention to the fact that *you are both sinners*. (Will it help if I repeat myself?)

And here's the problem. Not only does sin disconnect us from fellowship with God, but it corrupts our nature, infecting us with chronic self-centeredness (Jeremiah 17:9; Mark 7:20-23; Colossians 1:21). Lurking within the recesses of every person's soul is the character cleverly labeled by comedian Brian Regan as the Me-Monster. This dark side of one's personality is the custodian of self-interest, and it doesn't take much of a challenge to provoke it to action. One Me-Monster might be an entertaining foil for stand-up comedy, but two Me-Monsters in competition—not so funny.

What that means is that even if you and yours have an accurate grasp of the purpose and nature of marriage (as described in chapter 5), you will inevitably experience frustration (at least) in your efforts to make it work. Because of the sinful condition of both spouses, every marriage has within it the seeds of its own destruction.

That's not to say that all married people are perpetually miserable. The image of God was damaged, but it was not destroyed. Husbands and wives are still capable of creating meaningful partnerships and enjoying loving companionship. But the struggle, so glaringly absent from pristine Eden, is real. Too many marriages don't survive the conflict, and it tinges the best of them.

Swing Slow, Sweet Pendulum

The Rebellion had one other impact on marriage that is perhaps less obvious: *it knocked marriage out of balance.*

When God created Team Humanity, Adam and Eve carried out the two functions of marriage—loving companionship and working partnership—in equilibrium. But when the tug-of-war for control entered the picture, that symmetry was lost as one function came to dominate the relationship at the expense of the other. Throughout history, marriages have been lopsided. Rather than benefitting from marriage as originally designed, spouses have experienced frustration caused by the virtual loss of one essential function.

Interestingly, the imbalance has not been uniform throughout the Story of Marriage. Like a slowly arcing pendulum, it started out at one end of the spectrum and swung completely to the other. And this historical curiosity affects you personally.

For centuries, the idea of a partnership-in-work dominated society's picture of marriage. From antiquity until the eighteenth century AD, mate selection was based more on physical strength, skills, and material assets than attractiveness or affection. This was due in part to the curse pronounced upon our physical environment (Genesis 3:17-19), requiring countless families to scrabble for survival. But it was reinforced by patriarchal social structures in which the authority of the husband/father over his wife and children was virtually absolute. The head-of-the-household was in charge of a kin-based labor force that worked together to eke out a living or, under better circumstances, to advance the economic and social standing of the family. Companionship took a backseat to productivity or was sought (especially by men) outside the confines of marriage.

This conception of marriage as an *economic unit* profoundly affected priorities in mate selection. Throughout most of history, the notion of a "soul mate" would have been nonsensical to those who were sizing up the prospects. What they were really in the market for was a work partner.[4] This perspective prevailed into the mid-1800s in the American West, as illustrated by this ad placed by a bachelor in an Arkansas newspaper:

> Any gal that got a bed, calico dress, coffee pot, and skillet, knows how to cut out britches, can make a hunting shirt, and knows how to take care of children, can have my services till death parts both of us.[5]

This view of marriage was *institutional.* It was recognized to be an established social structure that contributed to the propagation and stability of the extended family and the culture at large. Furthermore, virtually all marriages were arranged by the parents of the prospective husband and wife. The array of choices confronting contemporary singles could not have been even imagined.

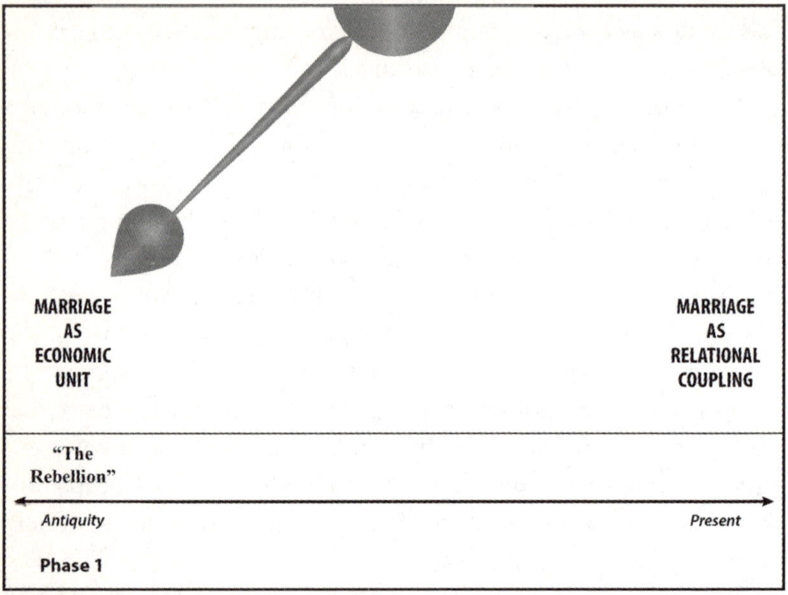

It's Thomas Jefferson's Fault

Do you remember reading in school about an intellectual movement of the seventeenth and eighteenth centuries known as the Enlightenment? It was a time when people began to challenge the prevailing authority of religious and political institutions. One expression of this challenge took the form of *individualism*.[6] For centuries, order had been preserved by requiring people to subject themselves to the social structures of the day. The survival and advancement of the extended family took precedence over the desires of spouses.

But gradually, a new appreciation for the value of individuals began to take hold. As it was famously enshrined in the American Declaration of Independence, "the pursuit of happiness" came to be regarded as an inalienable right of each person. When applied to mate selection, a relatively new criterion—mutual emotional fulfillment—was now being given consideration.

It didn't happen all at once, but over time the arranged marriage was replaced by individual freedom to choose or refuse a partner. Marriage historian Stephanie Coontz observes: "For the first time in five thousand years, marriage came to be seen as a private relationship between two individuals rather than one link in a larger system of political and economic alliances."[7] This represented a fundamental shift in the way people perceived the very nature of marriage. And over time, the role of romantic attraction grew in importance until it became the dominant factor in the choice of a spouse.

Another expression of individualism was the gradual exclusion of all parties other than the prospective spouses from the selection process. For a long time, even when parents were no longer arranging their children's marriages, their permission was still required. But by the middle of the twentieth century, parental blessing was becoming optional. The pendulum had swung to the opposite extreme from arranged marriages wherein a whole community was often engaged in the process. Increasingly, couples came to rely on their limited knowledge and experience with each other to make the most important and far-reaching decision of their adult life—in isolation from interference or guidance from others.

These two values—institutionalism and individualism—are not compatible. They were, in fact, on a collision course. But for a brief period following World War II, they coexisted in a balanced tension as the pendulum reached the center of its arc. Everyone understood and followed the same rules of dating and courtship. Virginity on the part of brides and grooms on the day of their wedding was a realistic ideal. Almost everyone got married and did so by the age of twenty-four. The husband went to work as the family breadwinner; the wife took over domestic responsibilities as a homemaker. They started having babies and raising a family.

That was the script when the authors of this book were growing up. Some call it "the Golden Age of Marriage," and just about everyone in America followed it. (I'm not suggesting that it was the right script; it was, in fact, flawed. But everyone seemed to be on the same page.)

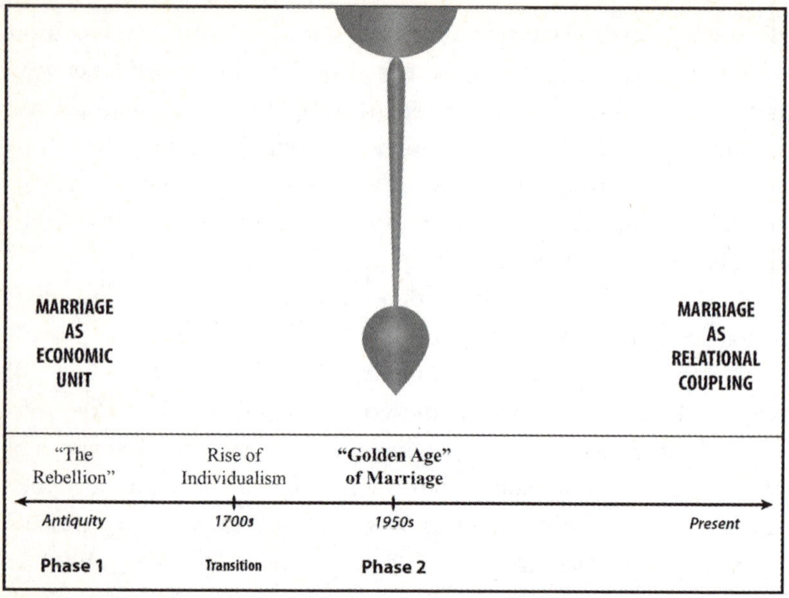

It's Our Fault

And then, in our teenage years, all hell broke loose. Our peers launched the Sexual Revolution. During the turbulent decade of the sixties, student radicals and hippies led the rebellion to overturn the prevailing standards, worldviews, and lifestyles of the Establishment. The development and accessibility of the Pill so reduced the fear of pregnancy that "free love" was pursued with reckless abandon. Under the influence of this movement, the ethical standards of the culture shifted 180 degrees in my lifetime. I can recall when there was a stigma attached to nonmarital sex, when girls who put out were considered loose.[8] Out-of-wedlock pregnancy was a cause for shame. Now virginity is stigmatized.

With hindsight we recognize that the seeds of the Sexual Revolution were sown in the era of the American Revolution. Inevitably, the increasing value of individualism challenged the priority of preserving a social institution. Something had to give. And what gave was the cultural consensus that had defined and supported the bonds of marriage.

Who Wants to Live in an Institution?

This change in the way many people came to view the very nature of marriage was a *really big deal.* What we have experienced is nothing less than the deinstitutionalization of marriage. Please read the following explanation by social scientists David Popenoe and Barbara Dafoe Whitehead carefully:

> The deinstitutionalization of marriage is one of the chief reasons why it is more fragile today. For most Americans, marriage is a "couples relationship" designed primarily to meet the sexual and emotional needs of the spouses. Increasingly, happiness in marriage is measured by each partner's sense of psychological well-being rather than the more traditional measures of getting ahead economically, boosting children up to a higher rung on the educational ladder than the parents, or following religious teachings on marriage. People tend to be puzzled or put off by the idea that marriage has purposes or benefits that extend beyond fulfilling individual adult needs for intimacy and satisfaction. In this respect, marriage is increasingly indistinguishable from other "intimate relationships" which are also evaluated on the basis of sexual and emotional satisfaction.[9]

As individualism began to conquer institutionalism, the swing of the pendulum away from a one-sided pursuit of economic partnership accelerated. The "couples relationship" is all about companionship. Everything else that used to be fundamental to our understanding of marriage has become secondary at best, even optional.

So as fallen mankind has tinkered with the definition of marriage, we have brought about significant change but hardly improvement. Now we have two problems. First, a primary function of marriage—the one that used to dominate social norms—is waning. We are in danger of losing the vision of marriage as a teamwork arrangement that makes a vital contribution to children, family, society, and ultimately the kingdom of God.

Second, the newly dominant function—relational companionship—has become corrupted in the process of its rise to prominence. Rather than a mutually up-building relationship based on a shared commitment to the sovereign rule of God, contemporary couples seek an arrangement that provides individual gratification. In the succinct statement of Timothy and Kathy Keller, "Marriage used to be about *us*, but now it is about *me*."[10]

Impossible Dreams

From this background and context we encounter our third modern myth: *Because marriage is fundamentally about companionship, the key to a successful marriage is to find and marry one's "soul mate."* Behind the search for the super-compatible spouse lies a drive to find a partner who will meet all my needs. This job description calls for a person who is physically attractive, socially appealing, and baggage-free. Not only does this person not need a lot of change ("low maintenance"), but he or she does not *require* a lot of change on the part of the suitor ("she accepts me as I am").

This way of thinking produces an idealized picture of marriage. Many singles in our culture look for a spouse to provide what only God can supply. So they end up requiring more of marriage than it can deliver.[11] Unrealistic expectations contribute to a fantasy that produces two unintended consequences. On the one hand, it prevents some singles from ever recognizing a suitable partner—even when a good prospect is in the neighborhood. On the other hand, it can cause an existing relationship to collapse under the weight of impossible dreams.

And most single persons have seen a lot of marital relationships collapse. This isn't just a matter of statistics. If they didn't grow up in a broken home, some of their friends did. Among their peers who have taken the plunge, they know several whose marriages didn't make it. Whether directly or indirectly, they have experienced the pain of divorce. And it has left a psychic bruise. So singles today are conflicted—pulled by their fantasies toward the hope of a marriage too good to be true and pushed by their fears of catastrophe too horrible to risk.

Trial Run or "Marriage Lite"?

Having lost sight of what marriage is for, and being apprehensive over what they are afraid it might become, singles have begun to take drastic measures in an attempt to ensure that their marriage will be what they would like it to be. The most radical of these ideas is the less-than-marriage arrangement known as cohabitation. A practice that has been regarded as taboo by virtually every civilization in every previous generation[12] has gained acceptability in contemporary western culture.[13] And so Christian singles are challenged by our fourth modern myth: *The best way to determine compatibility with a prospective mate is to live together.*

Jay believed this myth and acted on his belief. The distinguishing feature of his live-in relationship with Cindy was the absence of commitment. The tacit understanding of the partners in this arrangement is that either of them can leave at any time for any reason. Some cohabiters, like Jay, view their experience as a prelude to marriage—a time to test compatibility and get to know the other person in the context of everyday life. Indeed, cohabitation precedes marriage for over 60 percent of singles who eventually tie the knot.[14]

Others, like Cindy, take a more open-ended view, regarding their arrangement as an alternative to marriage that is less confining. Living with someone grants regular access to a sexual partner and a sharer in living expenses while allowing both participants to keep their options open. (It is not unusual for cohabiting partners to have different opinions on whether their current arrangement is preparatory or ultimate—often without knowing it.)

So now, instead of a universally accepted, uniform approach to courtship and marriage, *two* parallel *mating/dating patterns* are practiced in our culture. Some singles continue to pursue a modified version of the traditional courtship-and-marriage paradigm that prevailed during the first two-thirds of the twentieth century. But an alternative framework that is much less well-defined has arisen alongside the established one. Social historian Barbara Dafoe Whitehead calls it a "Relationships System." It is marked by flexibility and lack of commitment, and the "signature union" is cohabitation.[15]

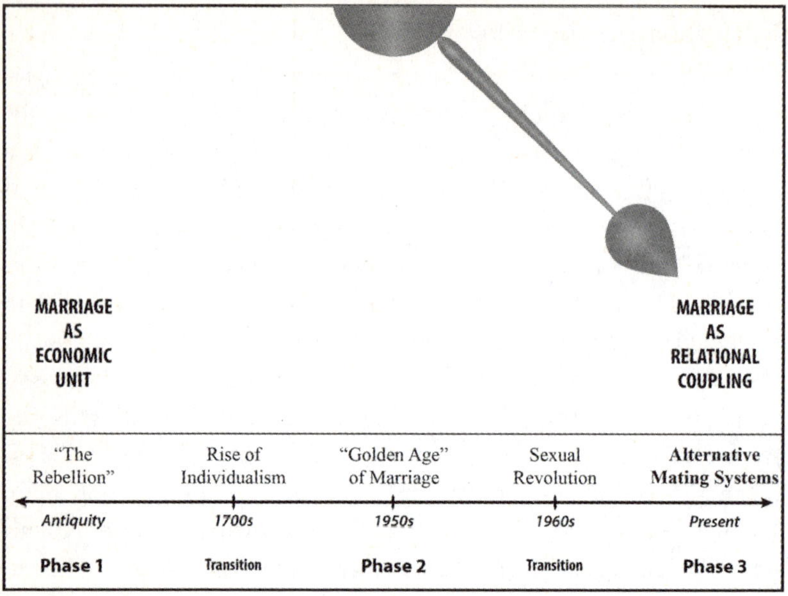

We will analyze cohabitation more in-depth in chapter 11. But for now, I will simply observe that because cohabitation is a distortion of God's design for men and women, it cannot accomplish what people hope to gain from it. It *is* a natural extension of the quest for a soul mate who will meet all of one's emotional and sexual needs and desires.[16] But this inherently self-protective, self-centered strategy more often fails to achieve what is hoped for.

Over half of cohabiting relationships do not transition into marriage but break up within fifteen months. And the hazard of divorce for cohabiters who do marry is substantially higher than for couples who have not lived together.[17] Furthermore, while both cohabiting partners grant the theoretical freedom to each other to leave the relationship with no strings attached, the pain of breakup for sexually entangled couples is scarcely less than that of divorce. Just ask Jay. Far from being a solution, cohabitation only contributes to the mess we're in.

To summarize: When mankind rebelled, marriage was corrupted. Instead of a relationship of harmony (companionship) and cooperation (partnership), the closeness became contaminated by conflict.

This strife was caused by a power struggle. From antiquity to modern times, the man dominated the woman by virtue of physical intimidation and his legal authority over her (granted and supported by the state or culture).[18] When the pendulum swung to the companionship extreme, the power struggle continued. Both partners have to satisfy the demands of the other in order to assure continuance of the relationship.[19] So now the power is held by the person in the relationship most likely to leave—whether by divorce or breaking up. (In the majority of cohabiting arrangements, this person is the man.) So the contemporary "solution" to the fear of marriage is a relationship characterized by fear of abandonment.

The Perfect Storm

In the introduction to this book, I made a statement that may have seemed exaggerated: *The venture of marital decision making is more complex today than it ever has been.* Perhaps now you can see what I mean. Since the Rebellion, the establishment of healthy marriages has always been undermined by the self-centeredness of the spouses and the corruption of the divine design for marriage. But now several elements have converged to create "the perfect storm":

- commitment to individualism
- deinstitutionalization of marriage
- evaporation of constraints on premarital sex
- increased sexual temptation due to later age for marriage[20]
- the divorce epidemic
- increasing acceptance of cohabitation
- rise of alternative "relationships systems"

As a result of these factors, the environment in which contemporary single adults are making marital decisions is nothing less than chaotic. Today there appears to be greater freedom and more options available to single people. But with the abandonment of older traditions, no normative guidelines have taken their place. Consequently, many single adults who would like to have a life-partner aren't clear about what form that relationship ought to take.

While established "mating rituals" of the past have been jettisoned, no definitive system has arisen to replace them. As one young man described the current dating scene, "You don't know whether you're going out for coffee or sex." So not only are unmarried people perplexed about the destination, they are also bewildered about how to get there. The result is widespread confusion and frustration.

The reach of this storm is immense. The number of people who find themselves in the same boat is stunning. Due to the ambivalence that never-married singles feel toward marriage, the prevalence of cohabitation, and the unrelenting plague of divorce, the sheer number of unmarried adults in our culture has reached unprecedented proportions. At this writing, "barely half of all adults in the United States—a record low—are currently married."[21] This dramatic demographic shift is but one more evidence that our contemporary efforts to reconfigure marriage have gone haywire.

••••••••

There is good news.

Act 2 takes us only halfway through the Story of Marriage. We have not been left to battle the elements on our own. The One who walked on water and quieted the tempest with a word has intervened to redeem marriage and those who are considering it. If you are looking for the happy ending, keep reading.

Don't Forget...

- Because of the self-centered inclinations of both spouses caused by sin, every marriage has within it the seeds of its own destruction. This is a reality that must be significantly and continually addressed.
- The cultural influences on mate selection today are the polar opposite of those shaping the marital landscape for

previous eras. Prior generations looked for a work mate; today's singles want a soul mate.

- Current western culture has endeavored to redefine marriage in terms of a "couples relationship." This approach has destabilized marriage as an institution and elevated the level of anxiety in the hearts of those considering marriage.
- Christian singles must realize that cultural conceptions of marriage represent a significant departure from God's design. They must also recognize that they are susceptible to societal influences in their decision making and take appropriate measures to guard against deception.

To access the endnotes and for questions for reflection and group discussion go to:

www.TheMarriageDecision.com

CHAPTER 7

Marriage: Jesus Remade It

Once there was a terrible accident. An alcohol-impaired driver lost control of the big truck he was driving. In his panic, he stepped on the accelerator instead of the brake and plowed into the living room of a home. Mercifully, no one was severely injured. But the damage to the house was extensive.

The little girl who lived there became distraught when she saw her bedroom in shambles. "Don't worry, Sally," her mother reassured her. "It will take a while, but we'll get your room repaired. It will be as good as new—maybe better."

The institution of marriage is like Sally's room. It got broken. But the wreckage we see is collateral damage from a larger catastrophe. Like the truck driver who violated the law against drinking and driving, our foreparents defied the ban on forbidden fruit. They lost their moral bearings, became spiritually impaired, and destroyed pretty much everything that mattered. They passed their impairment, and the ruined "house" in which they lived, along to us. Left to our own devices, we'd be stuck in a mess we can't fix. What we needed was rescue and recovery.

Project Re-Creation

Like the segments that preceded it, Act 3 in the Story of Marriage is a subplot in a much grander epic—the Drama of Redemption. In this act, the original Builder of the damaged creation dispatches his Son to repair and remodel what has been wrecked. To restore marriage, Jesus had to tackle the entire disaster created by the Rebellion. To fix marriage, he had to fix us.

In the deployment of Jesus to earth, God initiated an extreme makeover of the cosmos. In Act 3 of the Big Story, *God is acting in Christ to restore what was ruined, to reconcile what was alienated, and recover what was lost—especially human beings* (Luke 19:10; Acts 3:21; Romans 8:20-21; 2 Corinthians 5:17-19; Ephesians 1:3-14; Colossians 1:19-20). The end result of this enterprise will be the establishment of a redeemed community of people inhabiting a renewed, perfected earth, dwelling in eternal fellowship with and service to God (Revelation 21–22). This is the current project, and when it is accomplished (Act 4) it will take our breath away.[1]

Like most remodels, this venture is being carried out in stages.

Phase 1 is the part that every Christian is most familiar with. It is summed up in five precious words: "Christ died for our sins" (1 Corinthians 15:3). Theologians call this the work of Christ. In order to reestablish the connection between humankind and God that was broken by our transgression and guilt and to restore the marred image of God in our nature, the penalty of sin had to be paid. This was accomplished through Christ's atonement—his sacrificial death on the cross validated by his resurrection and exaltation.[2]

Phase 2 started on the Day of Pentecost and will continue until the project is completed. When he sent the Holy Spirit, Jesus created the community of faith, the church, to embody the rule of God and to recruit others to repent and join the fellowship of faith. Those who are reconciled to God through faith in Christ become "new creatures" who are not only born again, but also progressively transformed by the Holy Spirit into the *likeness* of their Creator (2 Corinthians 5:17; also 2 Corinthians 3:18; 4:16; Colossians 3:9-10; Titus 3:5). If you hear echoes of the activity of the original creation in this description, then you are correctly recognizing that this project is about the *re-creation* of what was so damaged by the Rebellion.

Now the divine remodel of all things includes "Sally's room"—the renewal of marriage. You will remember, perhaps, that the original purpose of marriage was to help the first image-bearers to carry out their mission to advance God's rule on the earth. In the re-creation project, Jesus *retrofitted* marriage to advance the mission of disciples in a fallen world. He recovered and restored believers' experience of marriage by three means: (1) his atoning sacrifice, (2) his teaching, and (3) his gift of the Holy Spirit.

Atoning Death: Jesus Redeemed Repentant Spouses

For husbands and wives to even have a shot at fulfilling their proper roles, something radical had to be done to solve the fundamental problem undermining their marriage. They had to be restored to a relationship of favor with their Creator. Then he, in turn, could bring about the renewal of character that would transform self-centered dispositions into other-serving hearts.

As we just noted, Jesus made the *provision* for this spiritual reversal through his death on the cross. The *means* by which repentant rebels are converted into beloved and obedient children is through faith (John 1:12; 3:16; Ephesians 2:8-10; 1 Peter 1:14-15). So the first and most crucial aspect of the restoration of marriage is the spiritual renewal of the participants. If you hope to participate in God's design for marriage, you must be born again.

Teaching: Jesus Retrofitted Marriage as a Ministry Institution

The reason that cultural conceptions of marriage in Act 2 deteriorated into distorted caricatures of the original is that self-centered spouses have attempted to redefine marital roles to their own advantage. In his teaching, Jesus clarified God's design for marriage in a fallen world. To reclaim that vision, would-be spouses need to note three key points in Christ's message.

First, in his rebuttal to Pharisaic antagonists in Matthew 19, Jesus *reaffirmed the validity of God's original pattern in a fallen world.* Even though marriages have become infected with "hardness of heart," God's people are expected to remain faithful to their marital covenants and pursue the blessings of a one-flesh union as God intended "from the beginning" (Matthew 19:3-9).[3]

Second, Jesus *put marriage (back) in its place as a component part of the larger spiritual family of God.* From the beginning, marriage was designed to establish the strongest bond of allegiance between two human beings. But that devotion was to be subservient to the spouses' higher commitment to God himself. When the Sovereign King was deposed, as it were, from his place of supremacy in the lives of the rebels, marriage assumed the position of highest loyalty for many people. Men and women turned to their mates to meet needs that only God can meet. Marriage became a vehicle for kingdom-building: the kingdom of self. Instead of being an avenue for serving God, marriage became an idol—the (un)holy grail that was sought to bring ultimate blessing and fulfillment.

Jesus encountered this reversed loyalty in people who claimed family obligations as an excuse for not following him (Luke 9:59-62). He challenged this subtle idolatry with the announcement that he had come to establish a new family, a spiritual one (Matthew 12:47-50). This was not a natural family entered by means of physical birth, but a supernatural family joined by means of regeneration through faith (John 1:11-12; 3:3; Galatians 3:7,26; 1 Peter 1:3-5), in which all distinctions of race or tribe are transcended (Ephesians 2:11-19; Colossians 3:11).

Then, in several provocative statements, Jesus made it clear that loyalty to him supersedes all family connections. Here are two examples:

> "Whoever loves father or mother more than me is not worthy of me, and whoever loves son or daughter more than me is not worthy of me" (Matthew 10:37).

> And Peter said, "Look, we have left everything we own to follow you!" Then Jesus said to them, "I tell you the truth, there is no one who has left home or wife or brothers or parents or children for the sake of God's kingdom who will not receive many times more in this age—and in the age to come, eternal life" (Luke 18:28-30).

This does not mean that marriage is irrelevant or unimportant in the scheme of things (as we have seen from Matthew 19). It does mean that marriage is not to be the most important thing to men and women. For disciples, Jesus demoted marriage from its place of primacy to a secondary status within the family of Christ, the kingdom of God—back where it belongs.

Jesus reinforced this corrected notion of marriage by elevating singleness to a status of significance equal to that of marriage within the kingdom of God. As we saw in chapter 3, he did this by his own example as a celibate man who ministered in a marriage-oriented culture, and by an explicit proclamation given to his disciples (Matthew 19:10-12).

If we were to envision all believers as an army, we might picture one battalion comprised of married disciples and another consisting of singles (the "special forces"). While they have different roles to play in the spiritual conflict, the essential pursuits of both groups must be understood in terms of the mission and purposes of the kingdom of God.

What we have seen about Jesus's teaching is that, (1) on the one hand, he *reaffirmed the validity of God's original pattern in a fallen world;* (2) on the other hand, Jesus *put marriage back in its place as a component part of the larger spiritual family of God.*

Finally, in his capacity as Sovereign King, Jesus *modified the original mission of his people* to correspond to his current project of re-creation. Rather than advancing the Creator's kingdom by "ruling over all the earth" as vice-regents (Genesis 1:26), Christ's followers are to advance the Redeemer's kingdom by *pursuing "above all" his rule and righteousness* as ambassadors (Matthew 6:33; 2 Corinthians 5:20). This revised mission establishes the overarching goal that is to govern every area of the disciple's life—including marriage.[4]

To sum up: In the teaching of Jesus, marriage continues to play a significant role in the lives of Christ's followers. But in a fallen world, *Christian husbands and wives are disciples first and spouses second.* The functions of marriage are to be harnessed in service to kingdom goals and priorities.[5] And the mission of advancing God's kingdom now focuses on the *spiritual* dimension of his rule not only in the world but also within the individual disciple.

GOD'S DESIGN FOR MARRIAGE

	In a Perfect World (Genesis 1–2)	**In a Fallen World** (NT)
Ruler:	Creator God	Redeemer God (Re-Creator)
Environment:	Pristine	Fallen/Hostile
Participants:	Image bearers	Disciples = Restored Image Bearers
Human nature:	Innocent	Fallen/Redeemed
Family:	Physically related	Spiritually related
Mission:	To serve God by advancing his rule throughout the world	To serve God by advancing his rule in my life and throughout my world
Functions:	Loving companionship Working partnership (including procreation of godly offspring)	LC and WP in service to The Great Commandment and The Great Commission
Priority of Allegiance:	A prior and higher commitment to the lordship of the Creator	A prior and higher commitment to the lordship of Christ

••••••••

There is a sense in which, during the Rebellion (Act 2), marriage got "too big." It usurped the place of God in the lives of human beings who required more of the institution than it could deliver. So Jesus had to pare it down, putting it in its proper place within the Kingdom of God.

But in the remodel of "Sally's room," the Contractor wasn't done. He wasn't satisfied with making it good as new. Through his gift of the Holy Spirit, he elevated the potential of what marriage could accomplish to a level previously unimagined. (We'll explore the implications of this gift for marriage in the next chapter.)

Marriage is not yet what it will be. But it can be better than it has ever been before.

Don't Forget...

- Jesus's remodel of marriage is part of his re-creation of all things.
- Through his atoning death, Jesus made provision for the spiritual rebirth and renewal of husbands and wives. This provision is the antidote to the destructive influence of sin that undermines marriages.
- In his teaching, Jesus
    1. reaffirmed the validity of God's original pattern in a fallen world
    2. put marriage back in its place as a component part of the larger spiritual family of God
    3. modified the original mission of his people to advance his rule and righteousness in their lives and their world
- In a fallen world, Christian husbands and wives are disciples first and spouses second. The functions of marriage (loving companionship and working partnership) are to serve kingdom goals and priorities.

To access the endnotes and for questions for reflection and group discussion go to:

www.TheMarriageDecision.com

Chapter 8

Better Than Ever

The auditorium was almost half empty by the time the worship team cycled through the final chorus of the praise song that ended the service. Here and there, knots of friends clustered together in earnest conversation. A couple of third-grade boys played tag among the rows of chairs as their parents debated which fast food restaurant should become their common after-church destination.

To all of this activity Jay was oblivious. He remained mesmerized by the chart on the page he was holding in his lap.

It had been six months since the wedding of his friends, Art and Becky, and his grandparents' fiftieth anniversary celebration. Three months later, he had joined a men's study group led by Art. Due to Jay's lingering depression over Cindy's defection, it had taken all of Art's persuasive powers to talk him into attending the first meeting. When it was announced that they would be studying the book *Singleness, Marriage, and the Will of God,* his immediate impulse was to bolt from the room. A divorced friend, Ted, convinced him to stick it out. "I'll do it if you will," he offered. "I figure I could use some reprogramming."

As a matter of fact, the study had been reshaping Jay's perspectives on marriage. The book's insights on the divine pattern were reinforced and often clarified by the group members as they batted around the discussion questions. Jay often found himself mulling the personal ramifications of the principles he was learning.

When Pastor John announced the beginning of a new sermon series on "God's Design for Marriage," Jay began to suspect a conspiracy. But the way the Sunday morning messages dovetailed with the midweek study had been nothing short of amazing. You'd think maybe they were coming from the same Source.

And then, this.

Today's sermon, "Three Models of Marriage," included a brief history of marriage. Pastor John demonstrated how human beings, in their rebellion against the Creator, have attempted to redefine marriage to fulfill self-centered desires. Then, in sharp contrast, he mapped out the elements of a "Spirit-filled marriage" from Ephesians 5. In the end, he compared three visions of marriage competing for acceptance in our world: Trending, Traditional, and Kingdom. To communicate the different perspectives of these three approaches, Pastor John set their characteristics side by side in a chart.

Jay normally appreciated Pastor John's charts, but this one affected him in a surprising way. It made his head spin. That's because the content provoked two epiphanies almost simultaneously. The first shed light on the recent past and, in an instant, transformed Jay's perception of Cindy's departure. What he had experienced as a disaster may have actually prevented one. The kind of marriage he had been hoping for with Cindy was now the one he most wanted to avoid. Her rejection of that relationship turned out to be a providential mercy, and he found himself shedding tears of relief.

The second flash of insight concerned the future. He had received a vision of what could be. His vague aspirations for a "happy marriage" had been displaced by a picture that came into focus with a clarity he could not have previously imagined. That such a relationship might even be possible boggled his mind. And yet he had it on good authority—none other than the apostle Paul—that this divinely revealed conception of marriage was intended to be the new normal.

"This," he reflected out loud, "changes everything."

Project Re-Creation Continued

If the marriage of a Christian couple was actually governed by the kingdom mission to advance God's rule and righteousness, what would it look like?

One way to frame this picture is by contrasting it to the situation we see in Act 2. In a previous chapter, I underscored the bad news about our fallen condition: namely, that within marriage, two sinners are placed within close proximity to each other for long stretches of time—with predictable and destructive consequences.

The good news from Act 3 is that a *Christian* marriage places two *redeemed* and *recovering* sinners into close proximity for long stretches of time. If these two individuals, who are strongly committed to each other, were to utilize the means of grace at their disposal, they could actually help each other grow! Indeed, by virtue of the intimacy afforded through marriage and the sheer quantity of time available for mutual edification, the marital relationship should enable each of them to be the *greatest human influence* for spiritual advancement in the life of the other. If that were to happen, marriage would serve as a vehicle for transformation—which is exactly what Jesus had in mind in his remodel of "Sally's room."

Jesus's Gift of the Spirit: A New Template for Marriage

In the previous chapter, I said that the Lord reconstructed our experience of marriage by three means: his atoning sacrifice, his teaching, and his gift of the Holy Spirit. The third provision is two-pronged: (1) revelation and (2) empowerment. That is, through new information communicated to his apostle, we have received advanced instruction on how marriage works for Christians in a fallen world (Ephesians 5:22-33). And through the ministry of the Holy Spirit, believing spouses receive divine enablement that transforms them from sovereigns into servants and empowers them to carry out their assignments (Ephesians 5:17-21).

Here is what the apostle Paul wrote to the Ephesian church:[1]

> Do not be foolish, but be wise by understanding what the Lord's will is...be filled by the Spirit...submitting to one another out of reverence for Christ.
>
> Wives, submit to your husbands as to the Lord, because the husband is the head of the wife as also Christ is the head of the church—he himself being the savior of the body. But as the church submits to Christ, so also wives should submit to their husbands in everything. Husbands, love your

> wives just as Christ loved the church and gave himself for her to sanctify her by cleansing her with the washing of the water by the word, so that he may present the church to himself as glorious—not having a stain or wrinkle, or any such blemish, but holy and blameless. In the same way husbands ought to love their wives as their own bodies. He who loves his wife loves himself. For no one has ever hated his own body but he feeds it and takes care of it, just as Christ also does the church, for we are members of his body. For this reason a man will leave his father and mother and will be joined to his wife, and the two will become one flesh. This mystery is great—but I am actually speaking with reference to Christ and the church. Nevertheless, each one of you must also love his own wife as he loves himself, and the wife must respect her husband (Ephesians 5:17,18,21-33).

In this classic passage, the apostle challenges Christian husbands and wives to relate to each other in ways that represent a reversal of our fallen impulses. Wives, who are influenced by the corrupting pull of sin to abandon their "helping" function and seek to control their husbands for their own selfish ends, are exhorted to respect and submit to their husbands. Husbands, who are influenced by the corrupting pull of sin to abuse their power, domineering their wives for their own selfish ends, are directed to love and sacrifice themselves for their wives. Instead of expending effort to get the other spouse to meet one's own needs, Christian husbands and wives are called to serve the other, to seek the other's good.

If this instruction consisted only of commands, it would mock us. For it directs us to act contrary to our sin-corrupted nature. But Paul does not say, "Just do it." Instead, he announces the availability of two Resources that can not only reverse the dynamics instigated by the Rebellion, but also elevate the constructive influence of marriage beyond anything previously imagined. These Resources—*Jesus* as the Master of both spouses and the Model of a sacrificial spouse, and the *Spirit* as the transformative power for servant-hearted ministry—were not available in this way to the generations of spouses who lived prior to the coming of Christ. The template for marriage established by Jesus (and described by Paul) was radically new, and its unveiling was accompanied by the spiritual dynamic that makes it attainable.

Who's in Charge?

To grasp the wonder of this message, we may have to refocus the lens through which this passage is often read. In the debate among Christians over "headship and submission," there is a tendency to view this paragraph as being about who's in charge within a marriage—who's going to lead and who's going to submit. In our preoccupation with the balance of power, it's easy to miss Paul's point. For the one thing that makes Spirit-filled marriage radically different is that *Jesus is in charge*. That is, Christian spouses are to respond to one another "out of reverence for Christ" (5:21) and "as to the Lord" (5:22) who, as the head of the church (5:23), is the supreme head of every marriage. His role in a Christian marriage changes everything.

You see, in most marriages, the point of orientation is the other spouse. The husband's treatment of his wife is most powerfully influenced by her attitudes toward him and vice versa. A man in love will do practically anything for his beloved. And that affection evokes kind and generous behavior—as long as it lasts. But when self-centeredness rears its ugly head, as it inevitably does, the pull of attraction is countered by the push of animosity. And the dynamic based on one's response to the other spouse can put the relationship in jeopardy. It is really difficult to serve the best interests of a person you strongly resent.

Paul never says, "Husbands, love your wives because they are so attractive." Or, "Wives, honor your husbands because they are such diligent providers." He always points beyond the other spouse to the One who stands over them both. In a Spirit-directed marriage, the point of orientation is Jesus. In fact, while this passage contains guidelines for Christian wives and husbands, that instruction is a secondary extension of the primary relationship between Christ and the church. Even when Paul quotes Genesis 2:24 as the summary description of the "mystery" of marriage,[2] he hastens to add "I am actually speaking with reference to Christ and the church" (5:32). What we are to understand is that human marriage is intended to be a *reflection* of Christ's marriage, which is the real thing. Our own marriages are not ultimately about us—they are about him.

When Christian spouses focus on Jesus, he influences their treatment of each other for good. Because he is their *Master*, they are motivated by gratitude to obey him. Because he is their *Model*, they are inspired by his self-giving spirit to imitate him. And his example helps Christian spouses at two levels.

First, Jesus models the *attitude* of sacrificial servanthood both husbands and wives are to demonstrate to each other. In the words "Christ loved the church and gave himself for her" (5:25), Paul draws us back to a vision of Jesus on the cross. Here husbands see the ultimate expression of "servant leadership" as the head of the church gives his life for his bride.[3] Wives, who are called to emulate the church in their submission to their husbands, may also draw inspiration from Jesus himself. For elsewhere, Paul points to Christ's sacrificial death as an example of submission to be followed by Christians who "in humility consider others as more important than [themselves]" (Philippians 2:3 HCSB).[4] This attitude, to which all Christians are called, is to especially characterize wives in their support of their husbands.

Second, Jesus demonstrates the *goal* of sacrificial servanthood. Husbands are to follow Christ who "loved the church and gave himself up for her to make her holy...and to present her to himself as a radiant church, without stain or wrinkle or any other blemish, but holy and blameless" (Ephesians 5:25-27 NIV). As Christ determined to do whatever was required to make the church, his bride, spiritually beautiful, so the husband should have similar commitments with respect to his wife. Pastor John Stott summarizes, "He will give himself for her, in order that she may develop her full potential under God and so become more completely herself."[5] Similarly, by her support and respect, the wife encourages her husband to be more like Christ as he seeks to fulfill his marital responsibilities. This goal corresponds precisely to the kingdom mission of spouses to advance the rule and righteousness of God in each other's lives.

The New Normal

If Jesus is the divine resource who is the point of reference as the Master and Model of marriage, the Spirit is the energizing power who inhabits the marital partners. He is the member of the Trinity who is dynamically present in the life of each believing spouse. Paul challenges husbands and wives to *be like Christ* in their attitude of servanthood and their goal of promoting holiness in the life of their partner. The Holy Spirit is the one who *makes us like Christ*, empowering us for godly living and transforming us into his likeness (Ephesians 4:16-19; see also 2 Corinthians 3:18; Galatians 5:16,25; Titus 3:5-6).

It is not surprising, then, that Paul's instruction to married believers is preceded by the prerequisite that makes obedience possible: "be filled by the Spirit" (5:18). Paul's succinct command is not some formula to be applied or a spiritual discipline to be enacted. It is a kind of shorthand for the spouses' attitude of reliance on the Spirit as they seek to carry out God's will within their marriage (5:17). As the Spirit's influence is brought to bear on husband and wives, they grow in their ability to reflect the character of Christ in the form of submission and loving servanthood.

Paul believes that the enabling power of the Spirit is stronger than the disabling influence of sin. He fully expects that the competitive impulses of Christian spouses will be conquered by Jesus's love and the Spirit's grace to such a degree that they will actively minister to each other in service to Christ.

In short, Paul expects that the kind of marriage he describes will actually be lived out by flawed human beings living in a fallen world.

And this vision of marriage is better than ever.

••••••••

Which "Game"?

We began part 3 with the premise, *you don't evaluate the players until you understand the game.* En route to this page, I have said there are three versions of "the game" competing for acceptance by couples today. Having tracked the developments of Act 2 and Act 3 in the Story of Marriage, you are now in a position to recognize and appreciate the related elements of these three alternatives.

Three Alternative Models of Marriage

	Trending	Traditional	Kingdom
Nature	Personal arrangement	Social institution	Ministry institution
Goal	Personal happiness	Mutual happiness	Growing holiness
Orientation	Self-oriented	Family-oriented	Kingdom-oriented
Driving question	How do I get my needs met?	How do we meet each other's needs?	How do we glorify God together?
Benefit	Self-benefit	Mutual benefit	Other benefit
View of spouse	Fulfiller	Companion	Teammate
Relation to spouse	Narcissistic	Reciprocal	Servanthood
Relational behavior	Manipulative	Give and take	Sacrificial
Relation to God	Autonomous	Acknowledging	Accountable/ Dependent
Experience of grace	Little (if any)	Common grace	Empowering grace
Role of church	Not a factor	Involvement included	Partnership
Threat of idolatry	Idol = Self	Idol = Marriage/ Family	No idol
Stability	Fragile	Stable but vulnerable	Strong
Longevity	"As long as love shall last."	Durable	Permanent
Stimulus	Spouse's devotion	Vows	Relationship to Christ
Modus Operandi	Self-fulfillment	Mutuality	Self-denial

The *trending* vision of marriage has evolved rapidly and recently in the wake of the sexual revolution. It fits consistently with a secular worldview not constrained by a religion-based morality. It has arisen as an expression of pervasive individualism, on the one hand, and as a reaction to the perceived limitations and failures of more traditional views of singleness and marriage. The dominant concern is the impact of a marriage on the fulfillment and happiness of the individual. This is the kind of marriage Jay and Cindy would likely have tried to implement had Cindy stayed in the relationship.

The *traditional* model views matrimony as a "permanent contractual union designed for the sake of mutual love, procreation, and protection."[6] While it is grounded in our country's religious heritage and thus serves Christians well, it is also the accepted framework of many couples for whom no spiritual component is important or necessary. Traditional spouses regard marriage as a social institution that exists for the benefit, not just of the husband and wife, but for children, families, and society as a whole. A marriage establishes a family, and the well-being of the whole is more important than the sum (or individual happiness) of its parts. Spouses count on the good-faith sincerity of the wedding vows and the consistent practice of mutuality for the success of the marriage, which is intended to be lifelong. Reasonably healthy, mature individuals of good character who implement the traditional model will usually experience a satisfying marriage. This is the paradigm practiced by Jay's grandparents and attempted by his parents.

The *kingdom* model of marriage views it within the framework of the spouses' relationship to God in Christ. They are disciples first, spouses second. They have a higher allegiance to their King, before whom they stand side-by-side. And their commitment to each other is an extension of that higher priority. Marriage is therefore a ministry institution serving the cause of the kingdom. The first focus of that ministry is internal—husband and wife each serving the other with sacrificial love to advance the rule of God in each other's life (i.e., spiritual growth in which the image of Christ becomes increasingly visible). Then, together as a team, they turn outward to advance the rule of God in the lives of their children and the world they inhabit. This is the model Jay now aspires to.

I trust it is evident that Christians are called to the kingdom model. The trending version is progressing further away from God's design. It offers to couples a formula for temporary euphoria followed by disappointment and disillusionment. The traditional model has enough elements of God's design to be serviceable. As beneficiaries of God's common grace, even unchurched couples who "get on the right side of how things work" experience the benefits of God's provision for humanity. But the traditional model lacks sufficient countermeasures for the damaging effects of sin. So it remains vulnerable to the corrosive influence of unresolved conflict. At its best, the traditional model falls short of what it could be.

The kingdom vision of marriage gathers up all the positive qualities of the traditional model and elevates them to a higher level. As believers pursue the kingdom model of marriage, the benefits of the traditional model are enhanced and the liabilities are eliminated. Spouses who share the traditional model at the time of their wedding can upgrade to the kingdom model as they learn about it. But it would be better to begin one's journey toward marriage with a clear picture of God's design.

Don't Forget...

- The upgraded template for marriage is energized by two Resources that had previously been unavailable to married couples: *Jesus* (the Master of both spouses and the Model of a sacrificial spouse) and the *Spirit* (the transformative power for servant-hearted ministry).
- In Spirit-filled marriages, the point of reference is Jesus. Rather than taking their cues only from each other, Christian spouses look beyond the other to Jesus. As Master, he motivates obedience; as Model he inspires imitation.
- By his example, Jesus models the ministry *goal* of

promoting holiness in the life of the beloved through an *attitude* of sacrificial servanthood.

- Through the filling of the Holy Spirit, believing spouses receive divine enablement that transforms them from sovereigns into servants and empowers them to carry out their assignments.
- Of the three available visions of marriage, only the kingdom model fulfills God's design for marriage in a fallen world.

••••••••

To access the endnotes and for questions for reflection and group discussion go to:

www.TheMarriageDecision.com

CHAPTER 9

Player Evaluation

Having decided to take more initiative to look for a husband, Nancy was following the counsel of the apostle Paul to evaluate the benefits and challenges of singleness and marriage. She identified some of the main pros and cons of singleness, and the difficulties that tend to characterize marriage. She had only to explore the advantages of marriage to complete her homework.

Her acceptance of that assignment coincided with the start-up of a women's group led by a newlywed by the name of Becky. They were studying the book *Singleness, Marriage, and the Will of God.* Nancy was also taking notes from a sermon series by Pastor John on "God's Design for Marriage." His most recent message on "Three Models of Marriage" was an inspiring eye-opener.

Nancy went home, found her journal, and completed the graph comparing singleness and marriage.

	Singleness	Marriage
Benefits	Freedom and flexibility Diverse and deep friendships	Sexual intimacy Complementary partnership with another in spiritual edification, kingdom ministry, and life
Challenges	Vulnerability to loneliness Denial of sexual intimacy	Challenges of making marriage work Diversion from "undistracted" devotion to God

From the outset of this project, Nancy's preference had been for marriage. That was still the case, but her perspective had changed in significant ways. For instance, she now had an appreciation for the favorable aspects of her single state. If God, in his sovereign purposes, intended that she remain single—whether for a season or a lifetime—she would trust that her experience of his grace would bring fulfillment to her life and blessing through her to others.

Her picture of marriage had also undergone major renovation. As she listened to the sermon on the "Three Models of Marriage," she realized that while she would not have consciously chosen the trending model, some of her expectations had been influenced by cultural values. Then when Pastor John described the traditional version, she thought to herself, *That's what I've been hoping for*. But the vision of the kingdom model expanded her imagination of what could be. *Heavenly Father*, she found herself praying, *if you grant my desire to marry, may I have the honor of loving you, ministering to my husband, and serving you with my husband in this way.*

Of course this vision of marriage also altered her perspectives on the characteristics she would now seek in a spouse. At the outset, she had been thinking in terms of a soul mate. But the presentation on the history of marriage challenged her to reevaluate what she was looking for.

Marital Functions: Restoring the Balance

In chapter 6, I chronicled the historic pendulum swing in societal conceptions of marriage from the Rebellion to the present. In Eden, the two divinely ordered functions of loving companionship and working partnership were exercised in equilibrium. After the Fall, the marital power struggle centered on economic concerns at the expense of companionship. But today, marriage is all about relationship with comparatively little concern for a working partnership.

With the coming of Jesus and his gift of the Spirit, Christian couples are called to restore the balance between relationship and work. This renovation entails two steps. First, we must counter our culture's distorted preoccupation with the quest for ideal soul mate. And second, we must properly restore the dimension of vocational partnership to a Christian picture of marriage.

Debunking the Soul-Mate Myth

The biblical construct of marriage challenges the soul-mate myth at three points. We have addressed all three of them along the way, so it will suffice to summarize them here:

- *Myth*: "There is only one such person out there for each individual—as was the case for Adam and Eve." *Truth*: In 1 Corinthians 7, the apostle's guidelines for decision making presume that there are potentially multiple candidates who would make an acceptable mate.[1]
- *Myth*: "If I find my perfect match, we will live happily ever after." *Truth*: Duke professor Stanley Hauerwas injects a dose of reality with Hauerwas's Law: "You always marry the wrong person." Even the most compatible mate will be flawed—as are you! Instead of seeking to be matched to the ideal person, each individual should determine to become a godly spouse who will build up the soul of another. "The adventure of marriage is learning to love the person to whom you are married."[2]
- *Myth*: "Marriage is fundamentally about getting one's sexual and emotional needs met, so I need a soul mate." *Truth*: This assumption turns a legitimate desire into idolatry. And idols inevitably fail to deliver on their genie-like promises.

What I have been critiquing is our society's distortion of the companionship function of marriage. The marital union is indeed *one* of the means by which God meets the emotional, social, sexual, psychological, physical, and spiritual needs of his children (Philippians 4:19). But the biblical corrective to cultural narcissism is to remember that marriage is primarily a *ministry* institution contributing to the mission of God's kingdom.

Reclaiming Vocational Partnership

Ben Patterson, in his book *The Grand Essentials*, reflects the biblical balance between loving companionship and working partnership with this insight:

> There are two images of marriage in the Bible. One is very popular today, the other has all but been ignored. The first is of two people gazing into each other's eyes. It speaks of intimacy and deep personal encounter and dominates the modern imagination. Its fullest expression in the Bible is in the lovely Song of Solomon.
>
> There is a second message, equally biblical, and much in need today to balance the first. It is of two people gazing, not at each other, but in the same direction, shouldering the same burden. It speaks of work to do together that simply cannot be done well alone. Its fullest expression is found in the second chapter of Genesis.[3]

The outward gaze reflects a couple's commitment to "working partnership." So what is it? Surely the partnership of spouses would function within at least three arenas:

First, should God grant them the blessing of children, spouses can be partners in *parenthood*. In today's world, teaming up to disciple the children is countercultural at two points. For self-focused marriages, children are an intrusion that detract from the primary goals of intimacy and self-actualization.[4] Further, in some families, the care of the children is consigned to only one of the parents, usually the mother. Christian couples, by contrast, share in the *privilege* of parenting. And they view it as a means of fulfilling the Great Commission—first, in leading their children to faith in Christ, and then, in making them part of the team that reaches out in ministry to the world around them.

Second, Christian spouses can be partners in *ministry* as they exercise their gifts and fulfill their commitments to the mission of the church. In some cases, they may work together as colaborers in a shared venture. At other times, they will find ways to facilitate each other's distinctive contributions to the overall enterprise of the gospel.

Finally, Christian spouses can be partners in their *occupations*. The workplace is one sphere where Christians are to exercise their stewardship; marriage is another. The trick is to manage these two spheres so that our efforts are mutually contributive rather than competitive. This balancing act requires each spouse to keep their job subservient to the mission of the marriage. This means, negatively, that the occupational tail will not be allowed to wag the marital dog. Put differently, the person who is a success at work but a washout at home has failed in the mutually accepted mission. And it also means, positively, that each spouse will make every effort to utilize the opportunities provided by their job (whether within or outside the home) to advance the mission of the marriage—to be salt and light in the workplace.

If Adam and Eve provide the prototype for God's original design for marriage, perhaps the model for marriage in the fallen world would be Priscilla and Aquila (Acts 18:1-3,18-19,24-26; Romans 16:3-5a). Evicted from Rome by the edict of Emperor Claudius, they set up shop in Corinth. There they provided hospitality for the apostle Paul, a fellow tentmaker. Their partnership in ministry with Paul deepened to the point where they "risked their own necks" for him (Romans 16:4). When Paul moved on to Ephesus, they went with him. While there, they brought corrective instruction to the eloquent apologist, Apollos. When Paul departed Ephesus, Priscilla and Aquila stayed on, providing hospitality and leadership for the house-church that met in their home.

Here was a husband and wife who dedicated themselves to a calling greater than mutual satisfaction or tentmaking. They are always referred to together, never individually; they functioned as a team, as partners in a shared mission. Far more than soul mates, they could be described as "mission mates." The scope of their influence ranged from hospitality to biblical instruction to church leadership. Together they were good stewards of the gospel. In their marriage we see a pattern for God's design for vocational partnership. As Patterson says,

> Without this...image of [vocational partnership] guiding us, marriages become narcissistic and self-absorbed; and they often collapse under the weight of expectations heaped upon them. With it, our marriages can have the balance of both the inward and the outward perspective. When couples realize that there is more to marriage than personal fulfillment—that they have a work to do together for the glory of God—a fresh wind blows into their relationship. Happily, personal fulfillment is then given as a by-product of a larger activity; not the ever-elusive pot of gold to be sought at the end of the rainbow.[5]

Kingdom-Oriented Player Evaluation

In the movie *As Good as It Gets,* Melvin (played by Jack Nicholson) is an isolated, self-absorbed, obsessive-compulsive writer who somehow develops a relationship with his waitress, Carol (Helen Hunt). In their conversations, his best efforts to say the right thing often come out sounding like insults. On their first date, one of his thoughtless comments hurts her feelings. But she gives him the opportunity to redeem himself with a meaningful compliment to her. He thinks hard, sweating bullets. Finally, he explains that when she came into his life, he decided to start taking the medication prescribed by his shrink to improve his obsessive-compulsive disorder—even though he hates, *really hates* pills.

"I don't quite get how that's a compliment for me," Carol says.

Melvin explains: "You make me want to be a better man."

This scene illustrates the perspective of Christian writers Laura Smit and Tim and Kathy Keller as they offer insight on how "understanding the game" affects "evaluating the players." They demonstrate how the kingdom model of marriage reshapes one's thinking about a prospective spouse.

Writing as a single woman, Smit argues in *Loves Me, Loves Me Not* that a Christian should marry only if marriage will advance the rule and righteousness of God in their life. Such a priority will, in turn, establish certain criteria for mate selection.

> Christians should be free to marry if marriage will make them better Christians. It does seem, however, that singleness must be the default choice for a Christian, given the clear preference for singleness expressed in [1 Corinthians]... In other words, the burden of proof is on the decision to marry, not the decision to remain single. Christians should assume that they will be single unless and until they have a godly reason to marry. Christians should never marry out of insecurity, fear, a desire to escape the parental home, a need for affirmation, or a search for financial stability. *Christians should marry only those who enhance their ability to live Christlike lives, those able to be true partners in Christian service, those who give them a vision of the image of God and the glory of Christ.*[6]

In *The Meaning of Marriage*, the Kellers turn this perspective around. Instead of simply holding out for someone who will build you up in your Christian faith, they challenge the believer to look for *someone to invest in.*

> Within this Christian vision for marriage, here's what it means to fall in love. It is to look at another person and get a glimpse of the person God is creating, and to say, "I see who God is making you, and it excites me! I want to be part of that. I want to partner with you and God in the journey you are taking to his throne. And when we get there, I will look at your magnificence and say, 'I always knew you could be like this. I got glimpses of it on earth, but now look at you!'" Each spouse should see the great thing that Jesus is doing in the life of their mate through the Word, the gospel. Each spouse then should give him- or herself to be a vehicle for that work and envision the day that you will stand together before God, seeing each other presented in spotless beauty and glory.
>
> My wife, Kathy, often says that most people, when they are looking for a spouse, are looking for a finished statue

> when they should be looking for a wonderful block of marble. Not so you can create the kind of person you want, but rather because you see what kind of person Jesus is making. When Michelangelo was asked how he carved his magnificent David, his reply is reputed to have been, "I looked inside the marble and just took away the bits that weren't David." When looking for a marriage partner, each must be able to look inside the other and see what God is doing and be excited about being part of the process of liberating the emerging "new you."[7]

The Kellers emphasize looking for a spiritual "work in progress" to which you, in partnership with God, can meaningfully contribute. The insight of Laura Smit provides the counterbalance: It is perfectly legitimate to hope for someone who thinks about you in the same way—someone who has the capacity and desire to contribute to God's work in your life. Together Smit and the Kellers provide the biblical antidote to the futile quest for the ideal mate. Jesus invites Christian spouses to be his partners in helping to restore and enhance his image in the life of another treasured human being.

•••••••

With her upgraded vision of marriage guiding her, Nancy felt that the broad parameters of what she was looking for in a husband were in place.

Now she was ready to put together a plan.

Don't Forget...

- With the coming of Jesus and his gift of the Spirit, Christian spouses are called to restore the balance between loving companionship and working partnership.
- The culturally influenced quest for an ideal soul mate is a distortion of the companionship function of marriage.

Healthy companionship is focused more on giving than on getting.

- Christian spouses will be work partners in parenting, ministry, and their occupations.
- The kingdom model will affect mate selection for single believers. Prospects should be drawn to the work of God in each other's life in a way that evokes a desire to contribute to that work.

To access the endnotes and for questions for reflection and group discussion go to:

www.TheMarriageDecision.com

God's Design for Marriage
At-a-Glance

Definition: "Marriage is an exclusive heterosexual covenant between one man and one woman, ordained and sealed by God, preceded by a public leaving of parents, consummated in sexual union, issuing in a permanent mutually supportive partnership, and normally crowned by the gift of children" [John R.W. Stott].

Mission: to serve God by advancing his rule and righteousness within our lives and throughout our world (Genesis 1:27-28; Matthew 6:33).

Functions:

- working partnership (vocational: Genesis 1:27-28; Matthew 28:18-20; Acts 18:1-3,18-19,24-26; Romans 16:3-5a; 1 Corinthians 16:19).
- loving companionship (relational: Genesis 2:18,22-24; 4:1; Song of Songs; Ephesians 5:22-33; Titus 2:4).

Nature: a [re]union of two lives into "one flesh."

Pattern: Marriage begins with a decisive act of commitment and is sustained by unified, daily faithfulness to the covenant (Genesis 2:24).

GOD'S PATTERN: WEDDING ➔ MARRIAGE	
Wedding	Marriage
"Leave and cleave"	"Become one flesh"
Public covenant	Private consummation
Faithfulness promised	Faithfulness kept
Legal bound	Physically, emotionally bonded

Model: Christ and the church—his self-sacrificing initiative and her loyal submission (Ephesians 5:22-33).

Empowerment: The ministry of the Holy Spirit (Ephesians 5:18, 21).

The *History* of Marriage:

- God made it.
- We broke it.
- Jesus remade and retrofitted it.
- We will all experience it.

Fulfillment: Human marriage foreshadows the ultimate union between Christ and the church (Ephesians 5:31-32; 2 Corinthians 11:2; Revelation 19:7-9; 21:2,9-11).

Part 4

Looking for a Mate

INTRODUCTION TO PART 4

Looking for a Mate

You don't evaluate the players until you understand the game. Once you understand the game, you can start looking for a good teammate.

We've spent the last nine chapters spelling out the nature of the game—God's design for singleness, marriage, and decision making. And we've covered a lot of ground. If you want a good review of the Rules of the Game, just go back through the "Don't forget..." summary statements at the end of each chapter, which provide a suitable framework for the project at hand.

The freedom to formulate a plan to look for a mate was established by the apostle Paul in 1 Corinthians 7. In chapter 4, we noted that his side comment to slaves encouraging them to seize any opportunity for freedom (7:21) opened the door to singles to initiate plans that could lead to matrimony.[1]

Planning is a good idea. It is better to be proactive than reactive. It is wise to decide (in advance) with the mind what the heart is looking for. Establishing criteria for evaluating potential mates and devising a plan for meeting and courting a prospective spouse are advisable exercises. Given the life-determining impact of marriage, I am mystified why more people don't put out the effort to do this.

The chapters in this final section will explore the recommended elements of a plan. Up to this point, we have focused considerable effort on exposition and application of key biblical passages that address singleness, marriage, and decision making. But now we turn our attention to questions Scripture does not definitively address. The Bible does not prescribe a single approach to mate selection. So our search is not so much for the explicit moral will of God as it is for wisdom.

Doing It Wrong

One of the most practical ways to identify and avoid foolishness in decision making is to learn from the mistakes of others. That appears to be the point of the following proverbs:

> It is better to live on a corner of the housetop
> than in a house in company with a quarrelsome wife.
> (Proverbs 21:9)
>
> It is better to live in a desert land
> than with a quarrelsome and easily-provoked woman.
> (21:19)
>
> A foolish child is the ruin of his father,
> and a contentious wife is like a constant dripping.
> (19:13)
>
> A continual dripping on a rainy day
> and a contentious wife are alike.[2]
> (27:15)

In his book *Making Life Work,* Bill Hybels summarized his conclusions from these verses: "The first time I read the book of Proverbs, I was a little surprised by its straightforward manner in addressing the subject of marriage. After many years of study and analysis, I have concluded that the wisdom of Proverbs regarding the selection of a marriage partner can be condensed to four words: Don't mess it up."[3]

Thanks to the abundance of research by social scientists on marriage, we have a pretty good idea about what choices contribute to marital disharmony and failure. I have summarized these findings in chapters 10 and 11. I hope these words of warning will help you to not "mess it up."

Doing It Right

It's one thing to avoid mistakes; it's another thing to make good decisions. Where, we wonder, is reliable wisdom to be found? The Bible emphasizes the role of wise counselors.

> When there is no guidance a nation falls,
> but there is success in the abundance of counselors.
> (Proverbs 11:14)

> The one who associates with the wise grows wise,
> but a companion of fools suffers harm.
> (13:20)

> Plans fail when there is no counsel,
> but with abundant advisers they are established.
> (15:22)

One of the advantages of living in the modern world is that we have access to the wisdom of counselors who have written down their insights and published them in books and articles. This can be very helpful because these are people who have devoted much time and energy in acquiring expertise in areas where ordinary people need help. For every unmarried adult, the search for a prospective spouse is a new adventure in which he or she initially has no experience. Being a novice in addressing the most important decisions an adult will make ought to prompt one to seek guidance from those who know the ropes. This is no time to be reinventing the wheel.

As you consult with counselors, however, you need to keep three things in mind. First, wisdom is not revelation. The experts are not writing with divine authority, so you must be discerning in your evaluation of their input. Second, being human, the counselors don't always agree with each other in every area. Where there *is* unanimity, you should give that agreement considerable weight. Where there is divergence of opinion, you must carefully assess the reasons for the respective points of view. Third, the counselors cannot make your choices for you. They can make helpful suggestions, but in the end, you are responsible for your own decision making.

The chapters that follow represent my effort to summarize the key insights of experts in relationship formation and marriage. Some of their expertise is anecdotal—they have formed conclusions based on years of counseling experience. But a lot of what they have learned is based on research, which provides a more objective basis for the conclusions reached. Significantly, much of that research confirms the ancient wisdom found in the Scriptures. And so a good deal of the counsel offered in the following pages corresponds to and illustrates biblical principles.[4] And some of it offers practical advice on how to implement those principles. As far as I can tell, nothing that is suggested violates the moral will of God.

The personal circumstances of readers of this material will vary greatly. Since I cannot know the situation of each reader, I am addressing those who, like Nancy the schoolteacher, are starting their search from ground zero—they have no immediate prospects but are interested in finding one. If you are in a relationship, these chapters can help you evaluate how things are going and determine whether any midcourse corrections are called for.

Chapter 10

Top Ten Missteps to a Miserable Marriage

No one wants to have a miserable marriage. But what many do not realize is that certain choices, commonly made, frequently lead to that sad result. Experts who have studied the dynamics of human relationships and marriage have identified specific behaviors and conditions (called "risk factors") that yield highly predictable outcomes. If someone were to set out to create a miserable marriage, these steps would help them accomplish that goal.[1]

Misstep 1: Choose Your Spouse with Your Heart, Not Your Head

The very thing that draws two people together and makes them consider marriage—namely, romance—is often the greatest threat to wise decision making.

What I am about to write may persuade some readers that I am the Grinch who stole Valentine's Day. So I need to say, for the record, that I think romance is a great thing. I have been twice pierced by Cupid's arrows, and both times I found it to be an agreeable and beneficial experience. Tim Stafford once described a significant value of being in love: "Romantic feelings do, as if by magic, make us want to be what we ought to be: entirely giving, thoroughly concerned with someone other than ourselves and wondrously joyful."[2] I found that to be true. My own conviction is that the capacity for romance is a gift of the Creator's design that facilitates the process of one-flesh bonding in marriage.

But in a fallen world, that gift can be abused and misused to grievous ends. One problem with romantic feelings is that they alter the lover's perceptions of the beloved in ways that distort reality. People who are "madly"[3] in love are spellbound. While the objective of sound decision making is to make *wise* choices, that part of the person tasked with discernment—his mind—is operating with diminished capacity. That handicap is problematic in a culture where couples typically fall in love first and then decide whether to get married. Often individuals make what is arguably the most important decision of their adult life with impaired judgment.

The technical name for this condition is *twitterpation*.[4] As Owl described the affliction to Bambi and Thumper, "You're knocked for a loop. And you completely lose your head."[5]

People have known about this condition, and the problems it causes, for a very long time. Three times in the Old Testament Song of Songs, sexually mature adults are warned against "awakening" or "arousing" erotic impulses prematurely (2:7; 3:5; 8:4). In antiquity, that meant reserving one's romantic passions for marriage.

What ordinary people have been observing for millennia has been confirmed by the research of modern science. In his book *How to Avoid Marrying a Jerk,* John Van Epp summarizes:

> Through brain-imaging studies, researchers at University College London found that "feelings of love lead to a suppression of activity in the areas of the brain controlling critical thought. It seems that once we get close to a person, the brain decides the need to assess their character and personality is reduced."...In addition, massive releases of oxytocin, dopamine, and other hormones and neuropeptides in the brain create euphoric feelings that further cloud analytic judgments.[6]

Like all intoxicants, romance can become mind-altering in ways that overrule good judgment.

The chapters that follow are addressed to those seeking to bring some objectivity to marital choices. Christians are to make noncommanded decisions on the basis of wisdom. In the acquisition of wisdom, the mind must be fully engaged. This is more easily done *before* one falls in love. That is why I plead with unmarried Christians to read this book as a *preparation* for marital decision making—while you still have full use of your mind.

And what if you are already twitterpated? Well, we can't turn back the clock on that complication now, can we. You're going to need to manage your heart while you seek for wisdom with your mind. And that can be done, but it's not easy. You should assume that your objectivity is already compromised and bring in outside resources to help with evaluation. As I will elaborate later, you would benefit from the services of a reliable relationship advisor (or, better, a whole team of advisors) accompanying you on your quest. For seriously dating couples, I advocate working with a counselor or pastor in pre-engagement counseling.[7]

I have listed this misstep as Number One because this disorientation is probably the reason people stumble into the other hazardous mistakes. That is especially true for Misstep 2.

Corrective: If you want to be as happy on your twenty-fifth anniversary as you are on your wedding day, engage your mind in the process.

Misstep 2: Marry Someone Who Does Not Share Your Commitment to Christ

For generations, spiritual counselors have warned believers against becoming "unequally yoked" with unbelievers based on 2 Corinthians 6:14-16 and related passages:[8]

> Do not become partners with those who do not believe, for what partnership is there between righteousness and lawlessness, or what fellowship does light have with darkness? And what agreement does Christ have with Beliar? Or what does a believer share in common with an unbeliever? And what mutual agreement does the temple of God have with idols? For we are the temple of the living God.

While this passage is not directly addressing marriage, it certainly applies to that relationship. For marriage is the most binding of all human partnerships.[9] When a Christian marries a non-Christian, they sow the seeds of conflict and rule out the possibility that that marriage will fully accomplish its design. For a believer and an unbeliever are fundamentally divergent at the very core of their lives.

But the point I am making here goes well beyond the prohibition against mating with an unbeliever. When one considers God's design for marriage—its mission, purpose, and functions—it should be obvious that a shared and growing commitment to Christ on the part of both partners is essential. The misstep here involves more than ignoring God's moral will concerning marriage to an unbeliever. It elevates a short-term longing to fulfill one's emotional desires over the wisdom of waiting for a partner who has the spiritual maturity to pursue a godly marriage.[10]

Corrective: marry a committed Christian who is growing spiritually and who shares your vision for a kingdom-centered marriage.

Misstep 3: Marry Too Young

While it is legally permissible for older teenagers to marry, it is not wise. "Marrying as a teenager is the highest known risk factor for divorce. People who marry in their teens are two to three times more likely to divorce than people who marry in their twenties or older."[11]

The reasons for this stunning statistic are not hard to understand. In our culture, few human beings reach psychological maturity before age twenty-five. During their late teens and early twenties, young adults are engaged in the intense work of identity formation.[12] During such developmental flux, one doesn't know oneself well enough to choose a marriage partner, much less make a wise evaluation of someone else who is going through the same process. "One author said it is like shooting at a moving target from a spinning platform. It is nearly impossible."[13]

While there is debate on this point,[14] I agree with those counselors who maintain that it is a misstep to marry too young.[15] If you need a chronological guideline, this means postponing marriage beyond one's teens, at least. More important than a specific age, however, is maturity and the ability to function well in an adult world. So the *corrective* to marrying too young is, grow up first. Marriage is for adults.

Misstep 4: Marry Too Quickly

Any couple who, like Tom and Sandee, plan to marry after dating for only two or three months is demonstrating that they lack the very maturity required of marriage. They are long on fantasy, short on reality.

During the early stages of a relationship, both individuals are putting their best selves on display. Initial attraction can have an inebriating effect on the perceptions each is forming of the other. Any couple that has been going out for three months or less know each other only at the most superficial level.[16] In their book *The Ten Commandments of Dating,* Ben Young and Sam Adams conclude: "We're convinced that the number one reason couples divorce is not money, sex, or infidelity, but rather the decision to get married was made too quickly."[17]

Courtship should last long enough to have some problems and work through them; long enough to become "experts" on the subject of marriage—together; long enough for those who know you best to observe you together and help you evaluate.

Virtually all the authors I read who addressed this issue set a minimum of two years for an adequate courtship.[18] One speaker explains that if you meet a prospective mate in your midtwenties, it's as though you are stepping into a movie that has been running for a quarter of a century. It's going to take a while for you to get your bearings: to figure out the plot, to understand the history to this point, to become acquainted with the cast of characters, to appreciate the subtleties in the personality of the lead actors and how they relate to the other characters in the story.

The *corrective* to marrying too quickly is go slow. Don't be in a rush. You've got the rest of your life to live with your decision.

Misstep 5: Confine Your Courtship to a Narrow Range of Experiences

It would be possible for a couple to spend a lot of time together and still be ill-prepared for marriage. One way this occurs is through superficial dating experiences that are long on fantasy but short on authenticity. If a couple's exposure to each other occurs in the context of a romanticized dating environment—especially if they become entangled sexually—they experience a false sense of intimacy that fails to lay a solid foundation for marriage.

Married life is not played out on a stage. It is not lived out in ideal circumstances where imperfections are hidden behind makeup and wardrobe. So courtship should provide opportunities for a man and woman to get to truly know each other through a diversity of experiences and in a variety of settings. A couple needs to see each other at work and at worship as well as at play. They need to serve God together in challenging circumstances. They need to experience hardship together, resolve conflict, negotiate competing values, sort out financial issues, weather some storms. They should become well acquainted with each other's families and friends.

The *corrective*: Get to know each other through a variety of real-life encounters.

Misstep 6: Marry Too Eagerly

This mistake often lies behind the three preceding ones. There are several reasons why people are in too big a hurry to get married. In some cases the eagerness is founded on an unrealistic view of marriage—an illusion that is out of touch with the real world. The idea here is that "Love will conquer all."

Some are too eager to marry because they believe that marriage is going to extricate them from an undesirable situation and replace it with one they expect to be an improvement. The classic example of this is the woman seeking to escape the control of her parents. Others who are overeager hope that marriage will compensate for a disappointing childhood. Still others turn to marriage to solve problems of loneliness or brokenness.

People who pursue marriage driven by fantasy, fear, or need are going to the wrong place to get their expectations met.[19] They will be doomed to disappointment. Marriage seldom solves problems; it tends to magnify them.

The *corrective*: Acquire a grown-up, biblically based understanding of marriage, and get realistic.

Misstep 7: Marry to Please Someone Else

"So, when are you going to settle down and get married?"

Most external pressure on single adults to get married is well-meaning, and not all of it is verbalized—or even intended. Finding oneself in an adult Sunday school class populated by couples, or getting a wedding invitation or birth announcement from one of the old gang can make a person feel like the odd (wo)man out.

Do people get married just because others expect them to? Sadly, yes. Some people form their identity out of their need to make everyone else happy. Sometimes the person they are trying to please is the one they are dating. They go ahead with marriage because breaking up would hurt the other person's feelings. Not only is this need to please an unhealthy basis for a self-concept, it places the power for decision making into the hands of other people. This is a form of voluntary slavery, and the likely result will be a life-sentence in an institution ruled by regret.

So there are two problems with this misstep. The first is that the decision making is controlled by the wrong person(s). For a covenant to have legitimacy, both partners must give willing consent. Husband and wife must have the ego-strength to choose for themselves. And second, the motivation for such marriage decisions is misplaced. Valid reasons for marriage should emerge from a person's understanding of God's design for marriage plus a mature evaluation of their situation in life. It's OK to want to please others within reasonable bounds; it's not OK to allow others to control our decisions.

I hasten to add that a person should not err on the opposite side—failure to consult with others about marital decisions. Especially in matters of the heart, individuals need the counsel of family members and friends to identify blind spots in their relational perceptions. It's just that in the end, the decisions that potentially affect the remainder of one's adult life should be made by the person who has to live that life.

The *corrective*: Make deliberate, freely chosen decisions based on biblical reasons.

Misstep 8: Make Assumptions Rather Than Mutual Decisions About Marriage Expectations

Every newlywed comes into marriage with expectations. Some of these are conscious. For example, the typical husband believes that his wife will never change. (She will.) The wife, on the other hand, expects that her husband—in response to her persistent, loving correction—*will* change. (He won't.) Such expectations are so deeply held that writing this paragraph was probably an exercise in futility.

But most of our expectations are subconscious and, therefore, unspoken. These are usually shaped by the homes the husband and wife were raised in. All of us have a picture of how marriage works—or how we think it ought to work. That picture is formed mostly from watching our parents (or the adults we lived with) and how they related. Over the years, we've made mental notes about things we like and things we don't like about how our parents (and others) got along. And those notes have created a profile of the kind of marriage we hope to have. The faulty assumption here is that the person I'm getting married to is thinking pretty much the same way I am about how our marriage is going to work. Or the man meets his fiancée's parents, observes how they relate, and thinks to himself, *Surely she doesn't want our marriage to be like that.* And he's wrong.

The problem in the preceding paragraph lies in the phrase, *and thinks to himself.* What the man needs to do is *speak right out loud* to his fiancée and ask, "Do you want our marriage to be like that?"

The *corrective* to this misstep: Explore and discuss expectations before you marry. This is where premarital counseling becomes so important. Discussing expectations with a third party monitoring the conversation can be extremely valuable.[20] Also during courtship, watch the marriages of people that you know and analyze them together.

Misstep 9: Ignore Unaddressed Personality/Behavioral Problems

My mother, Willine, was a victim of incest. The sexual abuse occurred during her teens, but our family didn't know about it until Mom was in her forties. She had repressed the traumatic memories, and they didn't come to light until she almost died from a toxic reaction to medication she was taking for insomnia. Her subsequent engagement in the process of recovery was nothing short of heroic, and part of her legacy to her children and grandchildren is a spirit of courage, grace, and hope. But I can tell you that my mother's experience of abuse took a toll on her, my dad, and our family.

Because of my mother's experience, I have had a special interest in the emotional and relational needs of abused women. Though I am not a professional counselor, I have learned about the dynamics of relational injuries of various kinds and their impact on subsequent adult relationships. As a pastor, I have walked with husbands through the process of their wives' recovery. And here is what I can tell you: *people do not simply outgrow childhood trauma.*

Growing up in a severely dysfunctional home inculcates unhealthy patterns of responding to others that become deeply imbedded in a person's psyche. These ways of relating become so "normal" to the damaged person that they aren't aware that anything is askew. Some of these learned behaviors appear positive to outsiders—high achievement, an extraordinary sense of compassion, a remarkable sense of humor. But eventually the detrimental, counterproductive nature of these learned patterns emerges—and the long-term impact on a marriage can be powerfully negative.

A lot of wonderful people have troubled pasts. In fact, a recent study by the US Centers for Disease Control and Prevention reported that 60 percent of American adults say they had "difficult childhoods featuring abusive or troubled family members or parents who were absent due to separation or divorce."[21] Now the presence of problems should not automatically disqualify a person as a candidate for marriage. But if a troublesome history or a behavioral pattern comes to light, one should ask: Has this situation been adequately addressed?

I have in mind two broad categories of problems. The first consists of issues stemming from one's family of origin. You should be especially alert for the Big Three: divorce, addiction, and abuse. Here's the bad news: the risk of divorce for adult children of divorced parents, adult children of substance abusers (addicted to drugs or alcohol), and adult children who have been emotionally or physically abused is much higher than it is for the rest of the population.

Here's the good news: the systems that children from dysfunctional families learn and apply to life are widely understood by relationship experts and can be comprehended by ordinary people. If your father was an alcoholic, you can gain much insight into yourself and the other members of your family by reading a book about adult children of alcoholics. If your fiancée's parents were divorced, you and she can learn about how divorce affects children like herself by reading a book written for that audience. There's a lot of good help available.

But dealing with one's past can be painful. So some people choose to deny the reality of their injury, hoping that time alone will heal the wounds and dim the memory. Pardon my French, but this approach will bite you (and your marriage) in the derrière. Marriage is for grown-ups, and you and your prospective mate need to be mature enough to face the past together in order to maximize the potential for a bright and healthy future. And reading is a good (and relatively nonthreatening) way to begin.[22] It is also important to discuss these issues in premarital counseling. And if the effect of childhood wounding was severe, professional counseling may be required. (Restorative therapy is one of the best investments a person can make.)

The second red-flag category is troubling behavior or personality patterns. Is there any evidence of addiction in the other person? Is there any history of substance abuse? What have they done about it? Do you recognize any extremes in the person's personality—reactions such as jealousy, anger, or stubbornness? Is there inflexibility? Is there dishonesty or irresponsibility? Can the person you are thinking of marrying get a job and hold a job? (If they cannot now, they will not later.)

The best time to deal with such issues is prior to marriage.[23] Rather than correcting such problems, marriage usually exacerbates them. Any flaws you recognize in the other person during courtship will likely become worse rather than better under the stresses of marriage if they remain unresolved. Plus, the motivation for dealing with them will have diminished.

Recognizing any of these characteristics in a person's life does not disqualify that person as a candidate for marriage. Everyone has problems. The question is, have the problems been significantly addressed and substantially resolved by the grace of God? Has the person grown as a result of having dealt with their past? If the answer to these questions is yes, you may have found an excellent prospect for marriage. But an unwillingness to address personal issues is a clear indication that this person is not ready for marriage. And if you ignore this warning, you can count on doing some heavy-duty work in your marriage.

The *corrective*: Unpack the baggage. Bring the issues to resolution. Get involved in counseling if that's what you have to do. Or run for your life.

Misstep 10: Test Compatibility by Living Together

A growing number of people believe that one way to prevent the previous nine missteps is to make a trial run. Cohabitation is so pervasive and the issues are so complex, I'm devoting the next chapter to this subject. But so we don't have a blank space on the chart below, I submit this *corrective* for now: Make relational choices that are moral and wise.

TOP TEN MISSTEPS TO A MISERABLE MARRIAGE

Missteps	Correctives
1. *Choose your spouse with your heart, not your head.*	1. Engage your mind—preferably before you fall in love.
2. *Marry someone who does not share your commitment to Christ.*	2. Marry a committed, growing Christian who shares your vision for kingdom marriage.
3. *Marry too young.*	3. Grow up. Marriage is for grownups.
4. *Marry too quickly.*	4. Court slowly. Get to know each other well.
5. *Confine your courtship to a narrow range of experiences.*	5. Get to know each other through a variety of real-life encounters.
6. *Marry too eagerly.*	6. Acquire a grown-up, biblically based, realistic understanding of marriage.
7. *Marry to please someone else.*	7. Make freely chosen decisions based on biblical reasons.
8. *Make assumptions rather than mutual decisions about marriage expectations.*	8. Explore and pre-discuss expectations in premarital counseling.
9. *Ignore unaddressed personality/behavioral problems.*	9. Unpack the baggage and bring issues to resolution.
10. *Test compatibility by living together.*	10. Make relational choices that are moral and wise.

Get Healthy

When we step back and look at all ten missteps together, there are three clarifying points I need to make. The first is that all ten of these common mistakes should be taken seriously. This list is not like a pop quiz that is graded on the curve. A couple should not console themselves by saying, "Well, we're only doing three of those things, so that's not too bad." Any one of these missteps could have serious consequences for a future marriage. If you multiply the risk factors, you compound the likelihood of negative effects.

Having said that, anyone who stumbles into one or more of these errors is not inevitably doomed to a miserable marriage or divorce. The mistakes I've been talking about are called "risk factors," not "coffin nails." Drs. Markman, Stanley, and Blumberg explain:

> Our studies (and others) show that marital failure is predictable to a surprising degree, which means that for many couples, the seeds of divorce are present prior to marriage. It does not mean that we researchers are very good at predicting exactly which couples won't make it, but we have gotten pretty good at identifying the factors that greatly increase the odds of divorce.[24]

These missteps may not ruin a marriage, but they will likely result in marital stress that *will have to be addressed.* God's grace is sufficient, but it will be needed.

Finally (and most important), all ten missteps may be symptoms of a pervasive, underlying condition: emotional unhealth. Neil Clark Warren says, "In 75 to 80 percent of all marriages that eventually end in divorce or separation, at least one of the partners suffers from an emotional health deficiency."[25] When asked for his one word of advice to someone about to get married, Warren replied, "Get yourself healthy before you get yourself married." One of his mantras is: *"No marriage can ever be stronger than the emotional health of the least healthy partner"* (italics his).[26]

Les Parrott teamed up with Warren to write *Love the Life You Live,* a book that points the way to emotional health. They identify three hallmarks of wholeness: (1) a profound sense of significance; (2) a lifestyle of unswerving authenticity; and (3) an attitude of self-giving characterized by generosity, truthfulness, and kindness. "At the risk of sounding too colloquial on such a meaningful matter," they say, "you can also think of health and wholeness as getting right with God (significance), getting right with yourself (authenticity), and getting right with others (love)."[27]

The reader who suspects they might need to address emotional-health issues, either because of circumstances related to their upbringing (such as divorce, addiction, or abuse) or current relational problems that crop up, can begin that exploration by reading. (I call this bibliotherapy.) The books listed below (or at endnote 22) are a place to start. Your pastor can refer you to other counseling resources in your area.

Don't Forget...

- The "Top Ten Missteps to a Miserable Marriage" do not guarantee marital failure, but they typically lead to problems that undermine marital harmony and will have to be addressed.
- Romance impairs judgment. Twitterpation may well lead to other missteps that are detrimental.
- Most of the ten missteps are symptoms of either immaturity or relational dysfunction. Marriage is for grownups who are healthy enough to pursue God's design. It is better to address personal issues before marriage than after.

....

Recommended Reading

Love the Life You Live by Les Parrott and Neil Clark Warren (Tyndale, 2004).

Changes That Heal by Henry Cloud (Zondervan, 1997).

How People Grow by Henry Cloud and John Townsend (Zondervan, 2004).

Putting Your Past in Its Place by Stephen Viars (Harvest House, 2011).

To access the endnotes and for questions for reflection and group discussion go to:

www.TheMarriageDecision.com

CHAPTER 11

Cohabitation: The Un-Solution

MODERN MYTH 4

The best way to determine compatibility with a prospective mate is to live together.

When I assisted Garry Friesen in writing the original edition of *Decision Making and the Will of God* in the late 1970s, we devoted two chapters to singleness and marriage. But it never occurred to us to even mention cohabitation. That alternative was not on the radar screen of our target audience.

My, how things have changed!

It Seemed Like a Good Idea at the Time

Prior to 1970, cohabitation was rare. It was viewed as a deviant, often unlawful practice engaged in by people at the fringes of society. Today, cohabitation is widely regarded as a normal part of life in Western countries. A majority of people in these nations will live with someone they are not married to at some time in their lives. Most young people intend to cohabit en route to marriage or, increasingly, as an alternative to marriage.[1]

The speed and scope of this shift in perspective is nothing short of astounding. Consider these statistics of the Cohabitation Revolution:[2]

- Between 1960 and 2009, the number of couples cohabiting in the US increased more than fifteenfold.
- As of 2002, over half the women between the ages of twenty-five and forty-four had lived with an unmarried partner at some time. This number contrasts with 33 percent in 1987 and virtually none a century ago.
- Cohabitation precedes marriage over 60 percent of the time. This makes cohabitation the most common way couples in America begin life together.
- More than 40 percent of cohabiting couples have children; approximately 24 percent of children born in the US have unmarried parents who live together.

While the pace and breadth of this development has been dizzying, the reasons behind it are no mystery. In chapter 6, we traced the evolution of cultural perceptions of marriage from an economic partnership to a love relationship as individualism conquered institutionalism. The Sexual Revolution, with its dismissal of moral constraints on nonmarital sex and unprecedented accessibility to contraception and abortion, precipitated the Divorce Epidemic. Set free from the strict traditions of the past but traumatized by the marital failures of their parents, the children of divorce began to consider unconventional ways to avoid bringing similar upheaval on themselves or inflicting it on their kids.

This is the situation Jay found himself in. He, along with a whole lot of other people, wondered, "Wouldn't it make sense for a couple considering marriage to live together for a time to see if they are compatible?" The logic of this approach seemed unanswerable and promised to avert marital disaster. So Jay joined the company of those who decided yes. He invited Cindy to move in with him. The unconventional had become commonplace.[3]

While the practice of cohabitation is now widespread, the reasons people live with another person are diverse. Cohabitation is variously regarded as

- a convenient dating relationship (reduced expenses plus regular access to sex)
- an opportunity to test compatibility for marriage
- a prelude to marriage
- an alternative to marriage

So What's the Problem?

Our obvious concern with cohabitation is evaluating whether this practice has any place in the process by which believers explore their options. I have already listed acceptance of cohabitation as one of five myths in contemporary culture, and it is Number 10 in my lineup of "Top Ten Missteps to a Miserable Marriage." So my bottom-line conclusion is hardly going to surprise any perceptive reader.

But the case for a "compatibility trial" seems so compelling that we need to investigate more carefully the dynamics of cohabitation before signing off on an unexamined verdict. This is one of those places where Christians may be tempted to wonder whether the guidelines of an ancient book may be out of step with the realities of the modern world. The book of Proverbs confidently throws down the gauntlet—in two different places:

> There is a way that seems right to a person,
>   but its end is the way that leads to death.
> (Proverbs 14:12; 16:25)

> Trust in the LORD with all your heart,
>   and do not rely on your own understanding.
> Acknowledge him in all your ways,
>   and he will make your paths straight.
> Do not be wise in your own estimation;
>   fear the LORD and turn away from evil.
> This will bring healing to your body,
>   and refreshment to your inner self.
> (Proverbs 3:5-8)

Let's accept the challenge to place the wisdom of man alongside the wisdom of God to see not only *what* the Lord requires, but *why.*

In the remainder of this chapter, I will summarize the biblical evaluation of cohabitation and spell out the ramifications in three corollaries.

The Biblical Assessment

In our culture, cohabitation describes the living arrangement of two sexual partners who share a household without being married to each other. From a biblical perspective, *cohabitation is a corrupted hybrid of the two sanctioned states of celibate singleness and faithful marriage.* It seeks the autonomy of singleness and the sexual communion of marriage. While we may speak of "God's design for marriage," and "God's design for singleness," no corresponding divine approval and purpose exists for cohabitation.[4]

When we evaluate our options as Christians, we are to ask two questions of each alternative:

- Is it moral?
- Is it wise?

The first of these queries asks whether God has specifically addressed the issue at hand. Is there a command or a prohibition that comes into play? And while that is not the case with many of the missteps cited in chapter 10,[5] this one does have an explicit moral component. God has blessed sexual intercourse within marriage (1 Corinthians 7:3; 1 Timothy 4:1-5; Hebrews 13:3) and prohibited it outside of marriage.[6] Cohabitation includes sexual activity by two people who are not married, so it lies outside the moral will of God. It is sinful and a corruption of God's design for singleness. So it ought not to be an acceptable option for Christians.

Remember that the moral boundaries established by God are not arbitrary. They are an expression of his character and are given for our well-being.[7] Obedience is the means by which we express our love for him, our trust in his providential care, and our submission to his authority to rule our lives. Even if he never explained the reasons for his directives, obedience would be the appropriate response. But on this subject, God has given us the dignity of extensive explanation, even if he hasn't told us everything. When we consider the three corollaries that follow, we can recognize the wisdom of his guidance.

The corollaries address the relationship between cohabitation and marriage because cohabitation is the means by which couples seek to experience the benefits of marriage, test potential for marriage, or replace marriage.

Cohabitation: A Corrupted Hybrid

Corollary 1: Cohabitation compromises the ability of a couple to fulfill God's design for marriage.

Some couples move in together thinking they can experience the benefits of marriage without contending with the liabilities. But cohabitation is less than marriage; it differs both in its nature and its intent. For that reason, this corollary maintains that cohabitation will inevitably fail to deliver what could be experienced in marriage.

For instance, one of the main objectives of cohabitation is companionship. That is also one of the two main functions of marriage. Do cohabiters experience companionship? Yes, often they do. But the companionship that God has in mind for marriage includes the dynamic of positive spiritual influence—purposeful investment by which each partner helps the other become more like Christ. Cohabiters who are willing to ignore the moral will of God to be together are hardly in a position to promote spiritual growth in each other's lives. That kind of companionship is not what they're after.

As for a work partnership (the other function of marriage), cohabiters may devise a system for sharing household chores, but they are hardly teammates in the game of life. True partnership requires the one thing that cohabitation lacks—commitment. Cohabiters may occupy the same living space and live parallel lives, but the tentative nature of their arrangement destabilizes the ingredients required for a true partnership.

And so the basic *functions* that comprise the essence of God's design for marriage lie beyond the reach of cohabiters. Apart from meaningful promises, there can be no reliable expectations.

This inability of cohabitation to fulfill the functions of marriage should not be surprising since they pursue different, almost opposite *missions.* Cohabitation is about personal happiness; it views the relationship with another person as a means to secure one's own fulfillment and well-being. But the absence of binding obligation is also viewed as a requirement of happiness. So cohabiters are unwilling to surrender freedom to secure a permanent deal. Kingdom marriage, by contrast, seeks to advance the rule and righteousness of God in the life of another. Such a mission prompts spouses to sacrifice their own interests in service to the other. Cohabiters seek self-fulfillment; kingdom spouses practice self-denial. These opposite attitudes are the product of antithetical missions.

In what I have just said, I do not mean to paint all cohabiters as self-absorbed narcissists. I think most people are trying to figure out how to make the most out of life on the terms that make sense to them. Many cohabiting persons give and receive genuine love that is enjoyable and fulfilling. But there is a human longing for something that touches the soul more deeply that cohabitation is not configured to fulfill.

We were created with a need for relationship. What we all want in our lives is another person who knows us intimately, accepts us completely, and is committed to our well-being; someone who won't abandon us when they find out what we are really like. What we long for is unconditional love. This kind of love characterizes the heart of God. It is the love to which kingdom spouses are called and for which they are empowered by God's Spirit. It is a love that persists in giving regardless of the response of the other.

This is the kind of love that cohabiters cannot afford to give. In the absence of permanent commitment, live-in lovers are perpetually on trial. A level of performance must be maintained to sustain the relationship. The authenticity and vulnerability required for a soul-to-soul connection is too risky. The threat of rejection is too great. And so the deepest, most satisfying kind of intimacy people hunger for is pushed out of reach by the terms of the contract.

Only marriage can do what marriage was designed to do.

COHABITATION: A CORRUPTED HYBRID

Corollary 2: Cohabitation misappropriates sex from its God-ordained purposes for short-term, self-oriented ends and jeopardizes the fullest enjoyment of sex within a legitimate, future marriage.

When God gave mankind the gift of sexual intercourse, he carefully explained its purposes. For the fulfillment of those purposes, he established the relational structure of marriage. In God's design, sex and marriage go together. It is as though he built a corral to control and channel the formidable power of a magnificent stallion. "Inside the fence," he declared, "sex is great; outside the fence, sex is destructive. Keep it in the corral."

Inside the Fence

In order to grasp the force of Corollary 2, you have to know the God-ordained purposes for conjugal sex. In *Singleness, Marriage, and the Will of God,* I devoted a chapter to this subject. In this instance, a succinct summary will have to do. From various statements in Scripture, we can recognize three broad purposes.

1. Procreation: The Reproduction of Image-Bearers

In the Genesis account, the first recorded words of God to human beings were: "Be fruitful and multiply!" (Genesis 1:28). We must not overlook the fact that procreation is the first stated purpose for sex. What God had just done (producing creatures in his own image), married spouses are to replicate.[8]

2. The Experience and Expression of One-Flesh Union

This is the point Jesus was making when he quoted Genesis 2:24: "God said, 'For this reason a man will leave his father and mother and will be united with his wife, and the two will become one flesh.' So they are no longer two, but one flesh. Therefore what God has joined together, let no one separate" (Matthew 19:5-6). The notion of one-flesh unity was the basis for his teaching against divorce.

This broad purpose of "one-fleshedness" is experienced in five interrelated ways:

- *Relational union.* More than just a physical act, sex is to be an experience of communion with another person.
- *Complementary union.* By virtue of their distinctive natures and anatomy, men and women experience sex differently. As the man gives and the woman receives, they experience completion in ways that complement each other.
- *Union with distinctness.* Becoming one flesh is not fusion; it is the creation of a community that unites two people while preserving their individual identities.
- *Consummation and renewal of covenant.* Each experience of sexual union becomes the reenactment, reaffirmation, and symbolic embodiment of the marriage vow.
- *Physical joy in love.* Sex is not only the experience of pleasure but the giving of pleasure, and the physical delight is enhanced by emotional and spiritual connectedness.

3. Illumination: Experiencing God's Love Story Through Our Love Story

When the apostle Paul quoted Genesis 2:24 in Ephesians 5:31-32, he linked the phrase "and the two shall become on flesh" to Christ and the church. Doug Rosenau and Michael Todd Wilson summarize the significance of this mystery:

> Our sexuality was designed to be the greatest parable of the ultimate love story—God's great love for us. Sexual

> intercourse between husband and wife is to reflect God's love for us—pure, priceless, and protected from all who seek to destroy it... *God designed our love stories to tell his love story.*[9]

In a kingdom marriage, sexual intercourse enables a couple to experientially know the mysteries of our bridal relationship to Christ at levels that go beyond the intellect.

Outside the Fence

Cohabitation stands God's pattern for marriage on its head. In marriage, commitment precedes sexual consummation; in cohabitation, sexual intercourse precedes permanent commitment. Cohabitation rewrites Genesis 2:24: "For his own happiness, a man shall withdraw from his father and mother (and everyone else), move in with his girlfriend, and the two shall have illicit sex." Getting the sexual cart ahead of the covenant horse has at least two consequences: (1) it postpones commitment, often indefinitely; and (2) it reduces sex to something less than a one-flesh communion.

Most cohabiters are frankly oblivious to God's purposes for conjugal sex. At the most superficial level, some view it recreationally. It is an appetite to be indulged, a pleasure to be enjoyed. It doesn't have to mean anything. Others *want* it to mean something. As they hold a lover in romantic embrace, sex becomes an expression of passion—an experience that enhances the sense of relational closeness.

By design, sex *is* a meaning-laden activity. But its true significance can be experienced and expressed only within the framework for which it was intended—marriage. *The covenant imparts the meaning.* Apart from the covenant, the experience of sex will inevitably fall short of its fullest potential, failing to fulfill God's purposes.

1. No Offspring

Where there is no covenant, there is no place for *children*. Unmarried people who choose to live together tend to be focused on themselves. Pregnancy in a cohabiting relationship provokes a crisis. It is a crisis for the parents who must decide what they are going to do about a baby and whether they are going to stay together. It is a crisis for the child who is born into an inherently unstable family constellation.[10] The number one reason given by the Creator for the gift of sex is the last thing most cohabiters have in mind.

2. No One-Flesh Union

Where there is no covenant, two people may become joined physically and attached emotionally, but they will never arrive at the transcendent *oneness* of soul that God intended. The conditional nature of their love injects the dynamic of uncertainty into the experience. You cannot become one with someone whose devotion you must continually earn. You cannot be one with someone whose intentions you do not trust. You cannot be one with someone whose rejection you fear. Nonmarital sex mimics the one-flesh consummation by creating a *feeling* of closeness[11] that is negated by the equally strong feeling of vulnerability to getting hurt.

3. No Illumination

Where there is no covenant, there can be *no representation* of the union between Christ and the church. An illicit liaison cannot mirror a divine covenant. Nonmarital sex can only be a caricature of the intimate union spouses are intended to experience and reflect.

Without the commitment, sex cannot do what sex is supposed to do. In fact, much of the time, it works in the other direction—it actually becomes destructive of the relationship and the people within it. This happens when, over time, the feeling of closeness does not lead to increased commitment, and one or both participants become disillusioned by the emptiness of the act. Sex also becomes destructive when sex is used to manipulate the other person, either in an attempt to maintain the attachment or to extract a higher level of commitment from them. Manipulation does not promote intimacy; it pushes the other person away. Which is the opposite of what sex is supposed to do.

It is better to keep the horse inside the fence.

Cohabitation: A Corrupted Hybrid

Corollary 3: The dynamics of cohabitation undermine the intentions of the cohabiters making failure more likely than success.

In the 1970s, when the practice of cohabitation was beginning to spread, many social scientists expressed optimism about the potential benefits of this approach to mate selection.[12] But in the years that followed, as formal research was conducted on the impact of cohabitation on subsequent marriages, the data revealed an outcome that was very different from what they expected: "The results of research suggest that a strong negative association exists between premarital cohabitation and marital stability."[13] So startling and universal were these findings that researchers dubbed this dynamic "The Cohabitation Effect." Rather than improving the quality of an ensuing marriage and increasing the likelihood of marital success (the stated goal of many cohabiters), the outcomes trended in the opposite direction.[14]

The negative influence of cohabitation on subsequent marriage was both surprising and clear. Less clear was how to account for it. Some analysts have argued that it is not the experience of cohabitation that leads to marital stress, but rather the personal traits of individuals who make that life choice. Couples most likely to cohabit are younger, poorer, less educated, more secular, and have some experience of marital discord in their background. So these influences cannot be discounted. But research that has screened for such "selection effects" has found solid evidence of a causal connection between the *experience* of cohabitation and subsequent negative marital outcomes.

This actually makes sense. While a growing number of people have signed on to the notion that a trial run would be beneficial to a couple considering marriage, closer examination uncovers problems. Three seem obvious to me.

First, the idea of a trial is faulty simply because it is *impossible*.

G.J. Jenkins writes, "It is ironic that many people opt for cohabitation as a trial for marriage, because the one thing that you cannot have a trial for is a permanent relationship such as marriage."[15] Diane Sollee elaborates: "The problem is that studies have found that cohabitation isn't enough like marriage to be a good test. You are testing living together—being roommates—not being 'all in.'"[16]

The mentality of cohabiting partners and married spouses is completely different. Cohabiters are *testing* compatibility; spouses are *building* compatibility. Cohabiters focus on *obtaining satisfaction* from their partner; spouses focus on *giving satisfaction* to their partner. The dynamics of commitment are also opposite: "'Til death do us part" creates a very different relationship from "as long as I'm happy" or "until I get bored." Therefore, even a "successful" cohabitation is not a reliable predictor of a successful marriage.

Second, the idea that if the trial reveals incompatibility the participants can just go their separate ways is astoundingly naïve. Most cohabiting couples do not marry. And when one member of a sexually bonded couple leaves the relationship, the impact on the abandoned partner (at least) is wrenching. Jennifer Roback Morse provides this striking explanation:

> Many people imagine that living together before marriage resembles taking a car for a test drive. The "trial period" gives people a chance to discover whether they are compatible. This analogy seems so compelling that people are unable to interpret the mountains of data to the contrary. Here's the problem with the car analogy: the car doesn't have hurt feelings if the driver dumps it back at the used car lot and decides not to buy it. The analogy works great if you picture yourself as the driver. It stinks if you picture yourself as the car.[17]

Talk to Jay about what it's like to be a rejected car.

But the devastation of a breakup is not the end of the matter. When a sexually entangled liaison falls apart, the emotional damage has a way of intruding destructively into subsequent relationships. The collateral damage extends to other individuals not yet on the scene—any potential mates of the estranged and wounded cohabiters.

Finally, couples often carry into their marriages patterns of thinking and relating they learned during cohabitation—habits that can undermine a marriage. One example is practiced self-withholding. Jennifer Morse, author of *Smart Sex: Finding Life-Long Love in a Hook-Up World,* passes along insight gained the hard way:

> When people live together, and sleep together, without marriage, they put themselves in a position that is similar to the person being asked to give a blank check. They either hold back on their partner by not giving the full self in the sexual act and in their shared lives together. Or, they feel scared a lot of the time, wondering whether their partner will somehow take advantage of their vulnerability.
>
> No one can simulate self-giving. Half a commitment is no commitment. Cohabiting couples are likely to have one foot out the door, throughout the relationship. The members of a cohabiting couple practice holding back on one another. They rehearse not trusting. The social scientists that gather the data do not have an easy way to measure this kind of dynamic inside the relationship. In my view, this accounts for the disappointing results of cohabitation.

And then she adds:

> I am sorry to say that I learned this from experience. My husband and I lived together before we were married. It took us a long time to unlearn the habits of the heart that we built up during those cohabiting years.[18]

Cohabitation = Counterproductive

I could say more about cohabitation. My intention here has been to evaluate the suitability of cohabitation as a step in marital decision making. Can I declare that if you live with someone prior to tying the knot, that experience will bring about a miserable marriage? No, I can't. The generalized findings of research cannot predict or determine the outcome of any specific situation. They can identify risk factors and alert people to consequences that tend to be more prevalent with certain behaviors. But plenty of folks who have cohabited maintain that it did no harm to their marriage.

That said, the testimonies of couples who may have dodged a bullet cannot overturn the combined force of the conclusions presented here—both social and biblical. And those conclusions agree that, as a stage in marital decision making, cohabitation is *counterproductive*.

Remember our two questions: Is it moral? and Is it wise? There is substantial evidence that there are flaws in the cohabitation arrangement that make it more problematic than helpful. And the reason for that is that it violates God's design—both for singleness and marriage. *What is immoral is foolish.* That's why cohabitation is a misstep that will likely have damaging effects on a marriage.

And that's why you should not go there.

A Better Way

What is moral is wise.

In the previous chapter, I suggested a correcting alternative to each misstep. In this case, the countermeasure to cohabitation is also the fourth key to effective decision making: make relational choices that are moral and wise.

I will expand on the specifics of such choices in the following chapters.

....

Postscript

The reason I presented the "Top Ten Missteps to a Miserable Marriage" in this and the preceding chapter is to help single adults *avoid* those mistakes in marital decision making. For some readers of this book, it may be too late to meet that objective for Misstep 10—you are already living with someone.

"What should I do now?" you may be wondering.

If you are interested, I have expressed my thoughts on that question in an article posted online at www.TheMarriageDecision.com. Go to "What Should I Do If I Am Cohabiting or Have Cohabited in the Past?"

Don't Forget...

- From a biblical perspective, cohabitation is a corrupted hybrid of the two sanctioned states of celibate singleness and faithful marriage.
- Cohabitation violates God's moral will and subverts his design for singleness.
- Cohabitation compromises the ability of a couple to fulfill God's design for marriage.
- Cohabitation misappropriates sex from its God-ordained purposes for short-term, self-oriented ends and jeopardizes the fullest enjoyment of sex within a legitimate, future marriage.
- The dynamics of cohabitation undermine the intentions of the cohabiters, making failure more likely than success.
- For those who aspire to a godly marriage, cohabitation is counterproductive. What is immoral is foolish; what is moral is wise—and beneficial.

....

Recommended Reading

The Ring Makes All the Difference: The Hidden Consequences of Cohabitation and the Strong Benefits of Marriage by Glenn T. Stanton (Moody Publishers, 2011).

Living Together: Myths, Risks and Answers by Mike McManus and Harriet McManus (Simon & Schuster, 2008).

Living Together: A Guide to Counseling Unmarried Couples by Jeff VanGoethem (Kregel Publications, 2005).

....

To access the endnotes and for questions for reflection and group discussion go to:

www.TheMarriageDecision.com

CHAPTER 12

Profile of a "Keeper"

MODERN MYTH 5

The most important criterion for a good marital match is chemistry.

God must have a sense of humor.

Do you recall my rant about the dangers of twitterpation in chapter 10? In my list of "Top Ten Missteps to a Miserable Marriage," Number One was: "Choose your spouse with your heart, not your head." It turns out I have some experience with that.

When I was in college, God, in his foreknowledge, knew that I would be writing a couple of books on marital decision making some decades hence. So he gave me the opportunity to do a little bit of personal research in advance. That education came in the form of a young lady—we'll call her Cathy.

Chemistry First

I met Cathy during the summer before my senior year, and she swept me off my feet. She was cute and vivacious and, for some reason, she set her sights on me. This was a classic instance of "Beauty and the Geek" (though we didn't use that word back then). And this geek was thoroughly, horribly, wonderfully twitterpated. It was a summer romance made in heaven. Of this I was certain.

So when I returned to college, I had this silly grin on my face and my feet weren't touching the ground. The photograph I was persuaded to display proved that Cathy was clearly out of my league. And it must have made my friends wonder, what does she see in him?

That, as it turned out, was a good question.

They say that "absence makes the heart grow fonder." They also say "out of sight, out of mind." Those two sayings are not compatible—one or the other will prove true. And for Cathy, the separation of two thousand miles and four months (with no e-mail, cell phones, texting, instant messaging, Skype, or any other social media) demonstrated the fragility of romance as a basis for lasting relationship. When I returned home for Christmas vacation, the fizz had gone out of the chemistry, and I found myself singing along with the Righteous Brothers, "You've lost that lovin' feelin'."

What in the world had happened?

I think a good case can be made for the theory that Cathy came to her senses. We were not, in fact, well-matched. They say[1] that opposites attract, and we were a case in point. Part of what Cathy saw in me (besides my innate charm and understated good looks) was my status as a leader in our Christian subculture. We were both Christians and we really hit it off, but we had precious little else in common. So lacking the time to cultivate the relationship, the magnetic force just petered out. (Also there was this other guy who came along who was actually handsome and had a nice car and didn't live two thousand miles away. So there's a competing theory that also has supporting evidence.)

The pain of rejection and the death of a dream were profoundly distressing to me. Yes, I had begun to formulate my thoughts about the future around Cathy. And I felt an acute sense of loss. It took several months before I could begin to appreciate how clouded my judgment had become. The mismatch had been clear as day to my grandfather—and probably a lot of other folks. But he was the one who *said something*. He wrote me a letter commending Cathy's many fine qualities, but he also carefully explained why she would not be a good mate for me. That was one of the most courageous acts of love I have personally experienced. Of course I disregarded his perspective at the time. (He was very old and not to be taken seriously.) But he was right. By the mercy of God and the severe kindness of Cathy, I was spared from a marriage that almost certainly would have had serious problems and may well have failed.

It took me four years to recover from my romance with Cathy, which was just long enough to get most of the way through seminary.

Relationship First

At the beginning of my senior year of seminary, I began to take stock of my prospects for life beyond the cloistered walls. I would need to get a job, probably as a pastor. Would a church hire a single man as a pastor? Hmmm. Maybe I should think about finding a wife. How would I go about doing that? What sort of woman should I be looking for?

My experience with Cathy had taught me that that last question was really important. And I actually knew the answer. By this time I had taken a course in marriage and family from Prof. Howard Hendricks. So I had made The List. Mostly it consisted of character qualities with commitment to Christ at the top. But it would be nice if she was musically inclined, physically attractive, and reared in a godly, healthy family. The List was important because I didn't want to give my heart to another person as I had with Cathy only to experience, or inflict, the kind of pain I had experienced when the romance broke up. In other words, I had no intention of starting something I couldn't finish.

I remember going for a walk one night and praying about my marital prospects. As I talked with God, I reviewed my List and used it to evaluate all the single women I knew who might conceivably be candidates for marriage. My goal was to winnow the field down to the Top Three. After thirty seconds of careful deliberation, I looked at the final cut and discovered only one name: Louise Bachman (real name).

I knew that Louise matched up well with my List because, over the last three years, she had become a good friend. Whenever I went home from school, we would spend time together—often working together to lead music for the college group in my home church. Not only did I enjoy her company, but I had reason to believe that she might welcome some personal interest from me.

As a candidate for marriage, she was almost perfect. In fact, there was only one drawback. On my part, the chemistry component was lacking. And I really wanted chemistry. So I pointed out this detail to the Lord. And I said to him, "If you can light that fire inside me, I'll explore this relationship and see where it goes." (Upon receipt of that request, the corridors of heaven were filled with gales of laughter as angels winged each other and chortled, "That poor sucker doesn't stand a chance." Yes, the angels *chortled.* It doesn't happen very often.)

Little did I know that I was the last character to make an entrance in a drama that had been playing for some time. For her part, Louise too had made a List. And somehow, my name had made it to the top of the pile. (After we were married, she showed me an entry she had made in her journal during a college retreat at which I had been speaking. It read, "Make a point to marry Robin Maxson." My amazement melted into chagrin when I noticed that this item was written in pencil! I am not making this up.)

For her, the trick was to get the attention of this man who was away at school three-fourths of every year and clueless about her considerable qualities when he was around. So she devised a strategy. When I was at home, she would place herself in close proximity through involvement with music. Most of the music we sang in those days was accompanied by guitars. She took the scholarship money she was awarded for being class valedictorian and bought a twelve-string guitar. She had the only twelve-string guitar in the college group. That put her on the worship team—right next to me. And she was a great guitarist.

When I was away at school, she wrote me letters and sent care packages on any holiday that provided an excuse. I appreciated this and said so in the *form* letters I sent back in response. (Yes, I know, I'm an idiot. Everybody has painful memories; this is one of mine.) She also courted, and won over, my entire family. When she spent a school term traveling around Europe and the Middle East, I didn't write to her—but my father did. If my parents had arranged my marriage, I would be married to the woman I am married to. Come to think of it, that's pretty much what happened. With Herculean patience, Louise worked her plan; and with corresponding restraint, my family allowed me to live under the delusion that I had some say in the outcome of what was about to unfold.

My little brother set and sprang the trap. A leader in his junior high youth group, he recruited me to be the speaker at their upcoming retreat between Christmas and New Year's. Then when he saw Louise at church, he said, "Are you coming to our snow camp? Robin is." So she signed on as a counselor. Somehow, through the process of planning meetings, prayer, conducting a retreat, sharing in trials and tribulations (junior highers, snow), and debriefing sessions, a spark was ignited. And the rest, as they say, is history.

I must add one more detail about Louise's plan that proved to be helpful. She took intentional, specific steps (that I will not detail here) to maximize her physical appearance—and the results were impressive. She herself had provided part of the answer to my prayer about chemistry. Suffice it to say, one of the great blessings of my life is that the lady who lights my fire is the woman I am married to. Amen.

Everyone's experience is different, but mine illustrates three themes that are prominent in this book. The first is the judgment-impairing effect of chemistry. John Epp calls it "that intoxicating attraction." And he passes along four warnings:

1. Chemistry is not always a good judge of character.
2. Chemistry sees what it wants to see.
3. Chemistry is not constant even in the best of relationships.
4. When chemistry precedes relationship, it prompts premature sexual involvement, which greatly complicates a relationship.[2]

If you are already enmeshed in a romantic relationship, there are two things I hope for you. In the opening pages of this book, I narrated Sherry's wish that her parents "had said something" about her mismatched connection with Eric. I hope that you have a parent (or a grandfather, as in my case) in your life who can help you recognize any red flags in your relationship. Several "grandfathers" would be better.

But there are two sides to this equation. My second hope is that you will be smarter than I was—that you will not disregard the counsel of anyone who knows you well and loves you enough to tell you something hard. If they are right, they may cause you grief in the short run but spare you from disaster in the long run.

The second theme illustrated in my experience is the preferability of relationship first, chemistry second. I will elaborate on that principle in the final chapter.

The List

The third point is the subject of the remainder of this chapter and the next: the benefit of developing a profile of the kind of person who would make a well-matched spouse—a "keeper."[3]

In a way, all of part 3—"God's Design for Marriage"—addresses this theme. That's because (say it with me), *You don't evaluate the players until you understand the game.* So we spent several chapters unpacking the dynamics of the game. If you joined Jay and Nancy in their respective commitments to pursue a kingdom marriage, you have already made some of the most critical decisions about mate selection. You are looking for someone...

- who shares your vision of what marriage is about—advancing the rule and righteousness of God
- who will be a companion in love and a partner in work
- in whose life God is working in ways that excite you and in which you want to make a meaningful investment
- who recognizes similar potential in you and has the capacity and desire to contribute to God's work in your life

So the most basic contours of a spousal profile are in place.

But now, since you are considering the person with whom you would be living, working, keeping house, spending money, sleeping, begetting and rearing children, and logging in time with his or her extended family, this needs to be a person you can stand to be around. Or better, enjoy being with. Mostly. What we're talking about here is *compatibility.* So it would be a good idea to sketch some additional details into the profile.

This is where The List comes into play. Virtually all the relationship counselors I read recommend the creation of a "shopping list" of criteria for a future spouse. For example, Neil Clark Warren recommends the careful and deliberate identification of one's top ten "must haves" as well as one's top ten "can't stands." Then he advises that the single adult adopt a no-compromise policy with those criteria. "Don't marry a person who doesn't have *all* of your top-ten 'must haves.' Similarly, don't marry a person who has *any* of your ten 'can't stands'." No exceptions.[4]

(This same counsel, in various forms, is given by H. Norman Wright, Ben Young and Samuel Adams, and Henry Cloud and John Townsend. Most of them offer a "starter list" so you don't have to begin with a blank sheet of paper. If you would like their help, check out this endnote.[5])

This is good advice that we apply in other areas of life. Whether we are choosing a college, shopping for a car, or looking for a place to live, we take the trouble to establish standards by which we will make an ultimate choice. Similarly, when the apostle Paul delegated the responsibility for the selection of elders to his protégés Timothy and Titus, he enumerated the specific qualities required of those who would lead Christ's church (1 Timothy 3; Titus 1). The profile he established continues to provide criteria for churches in their choice of spiritual leaders.

Taking the effort to carefully think through and write down our specifications for a spouse was very helpful to Louise and me. The resulting list contained criteria that we chose objectively before we engaged in the subjective evaluation of actual candidates. To be useful, such a list cannot be abstract and general; it must be specific.

Compatibility—Later Than Sooner

In the next chapter, we will explore key components of compatibility that ought (and ought not) to be included in a profile. But first, two personal observations.

First, I agree that compatibility, properly understood, is very important in marriages. As the prophet Amos famously said, "Can two walk together, unless they are agreed?" (3:3 NKJV). The two related functions of marriage—partnership and companionship—require being "capable of living together harmoniously or getting along well together; in agreement, combine well, etc.," as one dictionary defines *compatible*.[6] If compatibility is beneficial for any enterprise involving teamwork, it is especially advisable for marriage.

However, I also agree with Norman Wright's distinctive perspective on compatibility in marriage. In the second paragraph of his book *Finding the Right One for You*, he writes:

> Marriage. You want to be married or you wouldn't be reading this book. In fact, you're looking for that special someone who will be a wonderful companion, meet all of your needs, and totally complete you. *But you're not going to find such a person!* Every person you find will be flawed. But that's all right. All marriages begin with that condition. Keep searching, but realize that even with the best match you find, you won't really be 100 percent compatible in the beginning. However, you can *become* compatible. Plan on that as a major marriage goal for the first five to ten years.[7]

Later, he repeats: "You need the marriage relationship for the opportunity to learn to become compatible, and it takes the first decade of marriage for this to become a reality."[8]

I second that observation.[9] While a couple may attain a certain level of *affinity* during courtship, true compatibility is forged in the furnace of marriage. No matter how well matched you might be in temperament, background, values, interests and the like, one of you will be a man, the other will be a woman, and both of you will be (recovering) sinners. Making a good match should reduce the level of difficulty, but there will still be plenty of work to do in the process of *becoming* one flesh.

Is this nuance of meaning significant? I believe it is. For it alters what you are looking for as you evaluate prospective mates. Rather than assessing the presence or absence of compatibility, you ought to be appraising the *potential* for compatibility. This difference is subtle, to be sure, but important for two reasons. First, it injects a healthy dose of reality into the process. The existence of premarital harmony and chemistry do not guarantee success in the creation of a compatible marriage relationship. The task of building compatibility requires intentional, sustained effort on the part of both spouses. Second, it should help to refine your focus on what you should be looking for—the qualities that will *contribute* to compatibility.

One of the discoveries I have made in writing this book is that one of the things that distinguishes a *Christian* approach to marital decision making is asking the right questions. As you consider the desired criteria for a potential mate, you should use two questions:

1. What are the qualities of a person I could effectively join forces with in the pursuit of God's goals for our marriage?
2. What qualities in a candidate for marriage will contribute to compatibility?

Those are the right questions. And I think the answers to those two questions will significantly overlap.

....

Don't Forget...

- In isolation from other considerations, chemistry, by itself, can impair judgment about the suitability of a prospective mate.
- You should pay careful attention to a trustworthy counselor who expresses concerns about an existing relationship.
- To guard your heart in decision making, you should

carefully construct, in advance, a profile of a prospective mate—a list of required, preferred, and unacceptable characteristics.

- While compatibility is important in marriage, it is not something a couple starts out with but rather develops over time. In mate evaluation, you should be appraising potential for compatibility.

To access the endnotes and for questions for reflection and group discussion go to:

www.TheMarriageDecision.com

CHAPTER 13

Calculating Compatibility

The search for a mate is an exercise in risk assessment. The objective is to find another person whose characteristics maximize the likelihood of a successful marriage. I contend that this project is too important to be haphazard. I agree with those who advocate the creation of a profile of a "keeper"—preferably *before* you fall in love. Making a list of "must have" qualities, "can't stand" vices, and "desirable" bonus features could help you to recognize a keeper when you see one.

It wouldn't hurt, at this point, to pull out a sheet of paper (or boot up the computer) and start writing things down. But eventually you will find it helpful to organize the profile as five ingredients in the recipe for compatibility: character, commitment, comparability, complementarity, and chemistry.[1]

Categories of Compatibility

Character

In the introduction to part 4, I quoted verses from Proverbs on the unhappy plight of the man married to a quarrelsome or contentious woman. You will be glad to know that the writers of the Proverbs also expressed admiration for spouses of virtue.

> A noble wife is the crown of her husband,
> but the wife who acts shamefully is like rottenness in his bones.
>
> (Proverbs 12:4)

A house and wealth are inherited from parents,
but a prudent wife is from the Lord.
(Proverbs 19:14)

Who can find a wife of noble character?
For her value is far more than rubies.
(Proverbs 31:10)

One of the most useful case histories of mate selection in the Bible is recorded in the Old Testament book of Ruth. It tells the story of Boaz, a man who found a "wife of noble character" in an unusual way. After an unconventional courtship, *Ruth* was the one who proposed marriage![2] When he accepted her proposal, the reason he gave was that "everyone in the village knows that you are a *worthy* woman" (Ruth 3:11). ("Worthy" is the very same word as "noble character" in Proverbs 31:10.) The narration of their story gives a glimpse into what Boaz and Ruth saw in each other.

From observing her in the harvest fields, Boaz knew that Ruth was a hard worker. That was relevant because partnership in work is one of the primary functions of marriage. They both saw each other getting the yield of the ground from the sweat of their brows (Ruth 2; Proverbs 31:13-16). Further, Boaz witnessed Ruth's devotion to her mother-in-law, Naomi, a woman who described herself as "bitter" (Ruth 1:20; 2:11). Boaz concluded that if Ruth could love an embittered mother-in-law, she could love him, warts and all. As she worked in the fields, Ruth noted that Boaz cared for his workers, and they respected him as their foreman. Boaz and Ruth impressed each other with their diligence and their caring spirit. Finally, both were growing in faith. Boaz blessed Ruth for her faith, and his workers blessed Boaz for his faith (Ruth 2:4,12; Proverbs 31:28-29).

What Boaz and Ruth observed in each other's outward behavior was a reflection of who they were on the inside. Character is one's moral nature—those convictions and traits that guide one's attitudes, motives, and actions. A New Testament synonym is "godliness" (1 Timothy 4:8; 6:6; 2 Peter 1:3,6-7). *When considering a prospective mate, character is the most important category.*

The importance of character in the marital relationship is deeply imbedded in the very structure of God's design for marriage. As image-bearers, the first husband and wife were created and united to reflect the moral nature of their Creator. In a fallen world, one purpose of marriage is the growth of spiritual character in the lives of each family member. Each spouse is to intentionally build the other up in godliness. So it follows that the Christian single adult should be looking for someone of sufficient spiritual maturity and commitment to have the inclination and capacity to pursue those God-given purposes.

Further, character is that aspect of who we are that is most real and lasting. Counselor Henry Cloud says, "While you might be attracted to someone's 'outsides,' what you will experience over the long haul is their 'insides.' The only things that last are in a person's *character.* Or, I should say the only thing that makes a relationship able to last is a person's character." The biblical author who extolled the "wife of noble character" in Proverbs 31 implied the same point:

> Charm is deceitful and beauty is fleeting,
> but a woman who fears the LORD will be praised.
> (Proverbs 31:30)

Character is fleshed out in specific traits. The New Testament abounds in lists of desirable virtues: love, joy, peace, patience, kindness, goodness, faithfulness, gentleness, self-control, humility, compassion, integrity, forbearance, mercy, gratitude, endurance, contentment, generosity (Galatians 5:22-23; Ephesians 4:22-23; Colossians 3:12-17; 1 Timothy 3:1-7; 6:6,11,17-19; 2 Peter 1:5-8). Such a list may seem too abstract to be practical. But if you are trying to assess the character *of a specific person,* this inventory of spiritual qualities provides a ready-made checklist from a Reliable Source.

The Best and the Worst

In the estimation of relationship experts, certain virtues stand out as being especially valuable in marriage. In my research, the most frequently mentioned quality was *kindness.* Rabbi Dov Heller explains: "In Judaism we say that if you have two people who are kind, there is no possibility of divorce. That's because a kind person is a giver."[3]

Three other virtues emphasized by the Jewish counselors are humility, responsibility, and contentment.[4] Ben Young and Samuel Adams highlight five character qualities: faithful, honest, committed, forgiving, and giving.[5]

Another effective way to think about character is to reflect on what one *doesn't want* in a marriage. You don't want to be tied for life with someone who is *dishonest*. Trust is absolutely indispensable in marriage, and you cannot trust someone who lies or cheats. Nor should you commit to someone who has not learned to manage their *anger*. If your partner is *irresponsible*, you will spend your life picking up the slack. Neil Clark Warren warns against *obstreperousness*—"a big word for a person who is harsh, critical, unappreciative, difficult to please, and never satisfied. An obstreperous person will drain you of every ounce of energy you have and will make life a living hell."[6]

The profile you develop for a future spouse needs to give careful attention to the character dimension: What are your "must haves"? As you do this, a couple of things are important to remember. First, nobody's perfect. Anyone you consider will be a work-in-progress. A realistic standard is *relative* maturity. Presumably, a mature fifty-year-old will exhibit greater spiritual development than a mature twenty-five-year-old. The question is not, "Has he arrived?" The question is, "Where is he headed?" You are looking for red flags on the one hand and evidence of *growth in the direction of godliness* on the other.

Second, according to the Bible, the production of godly character is a joint-effort between God and the believer. The Christian is to take initiative to pursue Christ-like virtues (Ephesians 4:22-32; Colossians 3:12-17; 1 Timothy 6:11; 2 Timothy 2:22; 2 Peter 1:5-8). Yet any transformation that occurs is said to be "the fruit of the Spirit" that comes as we "remain" in Christ (John 15:1-8; Galatians 5:22-23; Colossians 3:9-10). So you should pay attention to *the priority a prospective spouse places on the cultivation of their personal relationship with God.*

Furthermore, since that relationship is best expressed and advanced in community, that person's involvement with a local church is highly relevant. Does she take initiative in engaging with God through spiritual disciplines such as Bible reading, prayer, corporate worship, and service? Does he have a group of Christian friends with whom he enjoys fellowship, experiences support and accountability, and engages in ministry? Does this person "seek first the kingdom of God and his righteousness" (Matthew 6:33) out of personal conviction and desire, or is their religious involvement dependent on you? In short, who is their God, and how do you know?

My sister-in-law, Elizabeth, experienced the disappointment of a failed first marriage. As she experienced sufficient healing to consider marriage again, she attended a presentation I gave at a church on decision making. During the question-and-answer session, someone asked for my take on the Bible's perspective on mate selection. Apparently I said: "Find the most spiritually mature person who will have you and marry them." I had forgotten about that comment. But Elizabeth wrote it down in the margin of her Bible next to 1 Corinthians 7:39-40. She took it to heart, and before long she found her Boaz. That advice was much more succinct than this book, but it worked for her. As of this writing, she and Terry have been happily married for over thirty years.

Commitment

This afternoon, as Michael and Cara stood before me in the front of the church, they looked better than they have ever looked before—and it's not just because they were wearing expensive clothes. They were, well, beaming. They exuded joy and enthusiasm and anticipation. They were getting married and they were so rapture-filled they were about to explode. Love and solemn decision making brought them to this place. But their hope for the future lay in the words of promise they recited to each other:

> I, Michael, take you, Cara, to be my lawful and
>   wedded wife.
> And before God and these witnesses,
> I promise to love you,
> To honor and cherish you,
> And leaving all others, cleave only to you.

And to be to you in all things a true and faithful husband
As long as we both shall live.

Marriage is a covenant between two people publicly declared. The willingness to stand before one's family and friends and make these *vows* is the fundamental factor that distinguishes marriage from cohabitation. One reason that husbands and wives become compatible is that, having made vows, no other option is entertained.[7] So while a bride and groom on their wedding day are deeply, gloriously in love, they are not counting on that euphoria to bind them together permanently. They are counting on something that is much stronger.

If Michael and Cara had pledged their vows in days of yore, they would likely have promised, "and thereunto, I plight thee my troth." When push comes to shove (or hopefully before), it is *troth* that keeps spouses together.[8] "Troth is an Old Eng[lish] word for fidelity, truth, trust, love and commitment…Keeping the troth is counting on each other, giving the utmost, sharing deeply from inside, sticking together through thick and thin."[9] It refers to the commitment of the covenant; it is synonymous with *cleave* (another Old English word) in Genesis 2:24. Romantic love flows from emotion; troth is a decision of the will. It is a promise that is as trustworthy as the character of the one who makes it.

This linkage between character and commitment ought to be obvious. And as you construct your profile, you need to be looking for someone who is a promise keeper. As a criterion for mate selection, reliability is a better indicator of marital stability than romance.

Comparability (Similarities) and Complementarity (Differences)

For years, one of Neil Warren's mantras has been: "Find a person to love who is a lot like you."[10] The short version of his recommended approach to evaluating prospects is this: "If you find somebody who has good character and is emotionally healthy, and then you get somebody who is a lot like you, the two of you will have a tremendous chance to make that relationship work."[11]

While other authors agree about the importance of substantial comparability, they collectively add important qualifications. First, don't misread Warren's advice to mean find somebody who is *exactly* like you. As John Van Epp explains, "[I]n most successful relationships, the two partners have a blend of similarities and differences in personalities, backgrounds, and lifestyles. The *balance* of this blend is what makes or breaks the couple."[12]

This balance is evident in God's original design. When God introduced Eve to Adam, his response was, "Wow! She's just like me—only different." There were ways in which she was comparable to Adam and ways that she was complementary. If the purposes of marriage are working partnership and loving companionship, then you're going to want your partner to be like you in ways that promote unity of purpose and perspective, while bringing distinctive characteristics and aptitudes that strengthen the team.

Constructive Similarities

When it comes to comparability, it's not just the number of similarities that counts but the *kind*. Some are more important than others. As you compile your profile, you will want to pay attention to five areas.

1. What matters to you

Values are the convictions and principles that guide the way we live and make decisions. *This is the most important category where you must be in accord.* Most relational conflicts can be traced to clashing values. Our values tend to operate below the surface, and most people would be hard pressed to identify their own. But you can uncover a person's values (including your own) through careful observation. How does he spend his time, energy, and money? What does she like to talk about? What makes him angry? What makes her happy or excited? What motivates him? What makes her bored? What does he praise? Your answers to those questions will expose many of a person's core values.

2. Where you have come from

As your two lives converge, the degree to which your *backgrounds* are similar will affect the ease with which you develop compatibility.

This includes your parental and extended family, culture, socioeconomic class, ethnicity, geographic setting, and religious upbringing. One of the reasons arranged marriages worked in bygone years is that these points of similarity were built in. If you have much divergence in any of these areas, you will have a lot of adjusting to do.

3. Where you are going

Our *goals* and dreams give direction to our lives. The questions here are: What do you hope to accomplish and what do you want to become? What are your respective goals for your education, your vocation, your family, your involvement in ministry, your financial security, and the like? These goals do not have to be identical, but they cannot be mutually exclusive. If you are going to be traveling together, you should have the same destination and be in agreement on the route you are taking to get there.

4. What you are like

Features of *personal makeup* where similarities are important include level of ambition, level of energy, level of intelligence (and even education),[13] sense of humor (do you laugh at the same things?), desire and ability for verbal intimacy, personal habits (punctuality, cleanliness, orderliness, social graces, weight management), work habits, and personal interests. These characteristics affect the level of comfort and enjoyment a couple finds in each other's company.[14] Since companionship is a major component of marriage, similarities in these areas (especially common interests) will advance the cause of compatibility.[15]

5. What you hope for

Your *expectations* of what your marriage will be like are shaped by the previous four categories. As I said in chapter 10, the expectations of each prospective spouse need to be identified and compared. Of particular importance is each person's assumptions about marital roles.[16] What will be the responsibilities of the husband? What are the anticipated duties of the wife? Does each person want children? How many? What parenting styles are preferred? Similar expectations bode well for compatibility. Dissonant expectations will produce a discordant marriage.

Complementary Differences

Earlier I said that it would be a mistake to be looking for someone who is *exactly* like you. Of course, there is no such person. Anyone you might find to marry will be significantly different from you in at least one respect—gender. As God was preparing to create the first woman, he said, "I will make a companion for him who corresponds to him" (Genesis 2:18). The word *corresponds* means "opposite" in the sense of "complementary." So the union of a man and a woman will, by definition, be characterized by substantive differences that are intended to strengthen the relationship. The whole is greater than the sum of its parts. As the French say, "Vive la différence!"

But other differences emerge as well. There is variety in the temperaments, aptitudes, skills, gifts, talents, abilities, and experiences that people bring to their relationships. In healthy friendships, families, and communities, we contribute our individual strengths to the well-being of others and are enriched in turn by those who have assets that we lack. This dynamic is particularly at work in a good marriage. In fact, we tend to be drawn to persons who possess what we do not have so that we can vicariously experience things that do not come naturally to us.[17] It is even possible to internalize and adopt the strengths of our partner as we become apprenticed to someone with distinctive capabilities.

Dangerous Differences

But not all our differences are complementary. Some are contradictory and others are potentially destructive. Almost all the relationship experts include a word of warning: "Beware when opposites attract." A normal appreciation for admirable distinctives becomes abnormal when one makes the opposing style or ability the *primary basis* for the relationship.

The problem with this kind of opposites-attract dynamic is that instead of fixing your emotional imbalance, you identify the opposite quality in someone else and think that *your relationship* will complete what is lacking. It doesn't! Instead, the relationship multiplies the problems and drives you further from center.[18]

Instead of a mutual relationship of love, an unhealthy dependency is established. In *Boundaries in Dating*, Henry Cloud and John Townsend assert, "Dependency that does not lead to growth ultimately creates more immaturity in the person."[19] And unfortunately, unbalanced people have a knack for finding each other: addicts find codependents, abusers find the victimized, controllers find adapters, and the emotionally needy find rescuers.

Other noncomplementary differences are less serious, but they will still bring challenges to a marriage. These are contradictory opposites that do not mesh well. Examples include the spendthrift and the tightwad or the social butterfly and the recluse. Such contradictory differences require negotiation and compromise on some middle ground that is less than satisfactory to either party. This sort of difference should be flagged before a couple makes a lifelong commitment. *If it bothers you when you're dating, it's going to drive you nuts when you're married.*

So how can you tell if a difference is complementary? Van Epp gives three helpful guidelines: (1) complementarity exists when time ends up refining the blend of differences in mutually beneficial ways; (2) this produces a deep and mutual appreciation of differences; and (3) partners with true complementarity become less different and more alike over time.[20] This is one evidence that they are *becoming* compatible.

Chemistry

Chemistry is a powerful feeling of attraction for another person. It isn't the same as friendship, for you can have all sorts of great friends who do not turn you on. It is a kind of emotional magnetism that draws two people toward each other. It creates the desire to be close, to hold hands, to kiss, to have sex. It is the sense of connectedness that is the *precondition* of falling in love.

When the experts on marital relationships talk about chemistry, there are common themes. The first is that no one knows what causes it. It appears to be a spontaneous response to a complex of factors that could include some combination of physical appearance, personality, sense of humor, charm, intellect, status, talents, spirituality, and the release of pheromones[21] (which, if true, would give *chemistry* another level of meaning). It is the most mysterious component in the recipe for compatibility.[22] "There are no 'Ten Steps to Developing Chemistry' with your partner. You either have it or you don't,"[23] some say.

(I'm not ready to sign on to such a sweeping generalization. If there is absolutely no chemistry to start with, the statement may be true. But if, to change the metaphor, there are embers, there are ways to blow on them if there is a good reason. Millions of couples whose marriages were arranged have started by "rubbing two sticks together" with highly satisfactory results.[24] And, as I found out, one can always pray. Still, there is enough truth in the generalization to pay attention to it.)

The second and third themes that emerge from discussions about chemistry are warnings. *Warning 1*: "Chemistry: don't get married without it." This may sound like a profound grasp of the obvious, for the assumption of most people (and even the Bible) is that people who are getting married can hardly wait to consummate the wedding. For most engaged couples, lack of chemistry isn't their biggest problem. But for some it is. Without violating the restriction of sexual union to marriage, you should be experiencing some symptoms of the urge to merge.

The more prevalent *Warning 2* is: "Don't get married because of chemistry alone." Neil Warren explains this caution well:

> While love without chemistry equals friendship, chemistry alone is not a foundational building block of your relationship. It is the icing, not the cake. If all you have is chemistry, that is not enough. Somebody said, "Passion, though a bad regulator, is a good spring." In other words, it is good at getting love going, but not so good at keeping it going. The chemistry of passion, without a base of deeper, more important compatibilities, typically lasts only about six to eight months.[25]

If chemistry is the icing, friendship is the cake. You need to *like* the one you love; or as Cloud and Townsend say, "Don't fall in love with someone you wouldn't be friends with."

> A real and lasting relationship must be built upon friendship first. You are going to spend a lot of time with that person. As one friend of mine said about picking her mate: "He was someone I knew I could grow old with. I liked spending time with him. And he made me laugh." She also shared deep spiritual values and other commonalities with him as well, as she would with any other friend. They have been married for nearly thirty years.[26]

The bottom line for the profiler: include chemistry and friendship on your list of "must haves."

FIVE KEYS TO COMPATIBILITY

Character: Godliness that is the product of a person's past-and-ongoing relationship with God reflected in specific, Christ-like virtues.

Commitment: Faithfulness to the marriage covenant underwritten by the reliability of the promise keeper.

Comparability: Similarities that promote unity of perspective and purpose

What matters to you—values

Where you come from—background

Where you are going—goals

What you are like—personal makeup

What you hope for—expectations

Complementarity: Differences that help each of you grow, to be better than either could be on your own.

Chemistry: A powerful feeling of attraction for another person.

The myth we are unmasking is the notion that "the most important criterion for a good marital match is chemistry." A lot of people think that chemistry equals compatibility—that it is the only thing that matters. The relationship advisors show us that compatibility is actually a constellation of elements that need to be taken into consideration. The actual equation looks more like this:

[Character + Commitment] +
[Comparability + Complementarity + Chemistry]
= Compatibility

The math nerds among us like this part. (Everyone else: this lasts for only one paragraph. Read it anyway. It's not that hard.). The brackets mark off subsets to show that the first two ingredients relate to each other in a distinctive way, as do the last three. Specifically, character and commitment are reflections of what a person is in himself or herself. By contrast, comparability, complementarity, and chemistry have to do with the characteristics of a person *in relation to* another.[27] The practical significance of these subdivisions will be spelled out below.

Sketching the Profile

When it comes to actually compiling The List, there are two extremes to avoid. The first is to create a profile that is too detailed, too idealistic. The mistake here is failure to distinguish between *requirements* and *preferences*. Some people put too many items from their "wish" list on their "gotta have" list. Or everything on the list is "gotta have." Overly idealistic specifications rule out everyone. You should be looking for someone who is suitable, someone to grow with. So figure out what is truly essential and leave some room for variation on your "hope for" list. You might be pleasantly surprised.

The opposite error is to compromise on the "must haves" and "can't stands." This happens when one settles for what is available rather than holding out for what really should be required. The idea behind the "must have" and "can't stand" lists is that every item included is nonnegotiable. Disqualification by a prospect on *any single criterion* is a dealbreaker. You're not grading on the curve—it's all or nothing.

This means you need to be precise in the construction of your "must have" and "can't stand" lists. It also means that most of the items on those lists should come from the first subset of character and commitment. Conversely, most of the items on your "like to have" list will come from the second subset of similarities, differences, and chemistry. (By the way, your specifications for those you will date and the person you will marry are not identical—see chapter 15.)

Are you going to make a list? I suspect that some who read this book will not bother—they will have too many other, more urgent things, on their plate. But I hope you will. Here's a suggestion: go on a one-day retreat and get it done. Study, reflect, and pray. Make rough drafts and then refine your profile to a finished product. Write your requirements in ink; write your preferences in pencil and keep an eraser handy. You will tweak your lists over time, maybe dramatically, as you grow. But you will find that it is helpful to have a place to start. And someday, you may want to show your profile to the person it eventually described.

How Does This Affect Me Personally?

As I conclude this chapter, there are two corollaries I must not neglect to mention. My focus has been on "the other person"—the theoretical marriage prospect. But this presentation on the ingredients that lead to compatibility has ramifications for the one making the lists. The first is this: if you are going to be evaluating similarities and differences, you must have a standard for comparison. And so the first corollary is: *Know thyself.* Before you can think of investigating someone else's assets and liabilities, you need to become an expert on yourself.

This principle becomes obvious the moment you begin exploring the areas of comparability and complementarity: background, goals, personal characteristics, values, and expectations. Do you know how your upbringing affects the way you live? Do you know where you want to go in life? Do you have ideas about how you plan to get there? Do you know your own inclinations and aptitudes, your abilities and gifts? Can you identify your interests and passions? Can you list the core values that motivate your actions and shape your decision making? Do you know your expectations of a future spouse or of yourself as a spouse?

This is why marriage is for grownups. One measure of mature adulthood is a sense of identity that is separate from your parents and your peers. Before you can take the measure of others, you must have some clarity on your own goals, values, convictions, interests, and expectations. So when you go on that one-day retreat, you may need to spend the morning sorting out your own profile.[28] And if you can't do that, you are not ready to consider joining your life to someone else.

With respect to the first subset, character and commitment, the second corollary is: *Become the profile.* In these areas, it is simply not reasonable to require qualities in a prospective mate that you do not have yourself. The ingredients that maximize the likelihood of building compatibility must characterize you as much as they do your future spouse, who may be looking for the very traits you would require in a teammate.

In a provocative article titled "The Question That Could Save Your Marriage Before It Begins," Les Parrott dares the reader to ask: "How would I like to be married to me?"[29] His point is one that many others have made. While it is important to find the right person to marry, it is more important to *be* the right person to marry.

Don't Forget...

- There are five ingredients in the recipe for compatibility: character, commitment, comparability, complementarity, and chemistry.
- The most important criterion for a good marital match is not chemistry, it is character.
- "Find somebody to marry who is a lot like you" (Neil Clark Warren).
- "Beware when opposites attract." Some differences are beneficial when they are complementary. But toxic differences are marriage-busters.
- Chemistry is important. But chemistry without friendship will not last. Marry a friend.

- When sketching the profile of a suitable mate, make a clear distinction between requirements and preferences. Don't compromise on your "must haves" and your "can't stands."
- To create a useful profile, you must know yourself well. To be a good prospect for someone else, you need to "become the profile."

....

RECOMMENDED READING

How to Avoid Falling in Love with a Jerk: The Foolproof Way to Follow Your Heart Without Losing Your Mind by John Van Epp (McGraw-Hill, 2008).

....

To access the endnotes and for questions for reflection and group discussion go to:

www.TheMarriageDecision.com

CHAPTER 14

Courtship: Crossing the Bridge

In *Get the Ring,* Sherry Zimmerman says, "Spouse hunting is very much like job hunting."

> Rosie and I suggest that our audiences approach the search for a dating partner—the kind of partner with whom they would like to develop a good relationship that can lead to marriage—the same way they would approach the search for a job.
>
> Let's say that my company was just taken over and my whole department was given pink slips. In two weeks I have to pack up my desk and move out to greener pastures. Will there be a greener pasture for me to go to? Not unless I make a major effort to find it. And so what do I do?
>
> I perfect my resume, I add information that is relevant to how my career has developed, and the kind of person I have become over the past few years. I polish my shoes, I make sure my suits look good, get a haircut. I network with everyone I know to let them understand what has happened and ask them if they can refer me to a firm or an individual who might be interested in hiring someone with my qualifications. I scan the want ads and I register with headhunters. I research background information about possible employers and I even practice how I am going to behave on a job interview. I try to be realistic. I know that I

> am not going to be hired on the first look-see. And I expect that if things are promising, I'll be called back a couple of times before the firm will make a decision. Nevertheless, even at the beginning, I try to make my best impression. I want to make my best effort to find the best possible job.[1]

Is that good counsel? Consider this wisdom from Proverbs 21:5 (NLT):

> Good planning and hard work lead to prosperity,
> but hasty shortcuts lead to poverty.

When it comes to marital decision making, I think many people want the process to be easy, and they want the outcome to be good. But that's not how life works. Prosperity is more often the product of "good planning and hard work."

On July 31, 1970, Louise Bachman made a note to herself in her journal: "Make a point to marry Robin Maxson." On November 10, 1973, she put a check mark next to that item on her to-do list. During the intervening months, she devised and executed the plan through which, ultimately, her desired outcome was attained. (Some aspects of her strategy and the way it unfolded are narrated in chapter 12.) When we married, I had no inkling that I would ever write a book like this. But it is certainly convenient that one of the best illustrations of its principles that I know is my own wife.

I do not mean to imply, of course, that those who create and implement an effective plan are assured of achieving their desires. As we saw in chapter 2, the ultimate determiner of such outcomes is the sovereign will of God. But I think there is good reason to believe that Louise's marital hopes would not have come about apart from her creative initiative. If you want to find a mate, you should have a profile and you should develop a plan.

Which Map?

If you are a single person who eventually marries, you will go through some process of progressive knowledge, attraction, and commitment to another person that culminates in a wedding. In Western culture, that process has been referred to as courtship. Courting has usually involved dating, a term sometimes used as a synonym, but is actually a distinct activity that may or may not be directly related to courtship.

In 2005, several Christian authors contributed to an anthology on courtship: *5 Paths to the Love of Your Life: Defining Your Dating Style.*[2] The metaphor of a journey seems apt enough. And given the complexities of human personalities, the dynamics of interpersonal relationships, and the mystery of love, it comes as no surprise that the venture of getting from Point A to Point M ranges from challenging to daunting. The title of that book is a tip-off that this matter has become a little complicated.

It has not always been thus. Throughout much of human history, a prospective bride was introduced to her chosen groom and that was that. The journey more or less began at the altar, and the hard work was reserved for the marriage itself. But our culture has opted for freedom of choice. And part of the price we pay for this do-it-yourself approach includes labor and anxiety and the risk of a broken heart. It's like climbing on a roller coaster with the hope that you don't have to get off before it reaches its destination.

For modern singles, navigating the terrain between singleness and matrimony has never been easy. But in recent years, it has become even harder. In the subculture of my youth, there was a prescribed route to marriage. But that is no longer the case. Writing in 2000, University of Chicago professors Amy and Leon Kass observed:

> Until what seems like only yesterday, young people were groomed for marriage, and the paths leading to it were culturally well set out, at least in rough outline...Today there are no socially prescribed forms of conduct that help guide young men and women in the direction of matrimony... For the great majority the way to the altar is uncharted territory. It's every couple on its own bottom, without a compass, often without a goal. Those who reach the altar seem to have stumbled on it by accident.[3]

As far as I can tell, in the ensuing decade plus, that situation has not improved.

If you are a single Christian looking for a mate, you have some important advantages over your secular counterparts. Because you understand God's design for marriage, you have a clearer picture of the *destination*. While the choice of whether to set out for that destination is yours, you have been given good *criteria* for making that decision. Unlike many of your peers, you do have a *compass* that can keep you from getting lost—the moral will of God. You also have access to trustworthy *guides* (wise mentors) who can help you find your way along the path. And you have a *Travel Agent* who guarantees your safe arrival at the destination of his choosing as he secretly guides by means of his sovereign will.

But what will you use for a *map*?

The professors Kass maintain that the map got lost. By contrast, the contributors to *5 Paths to the Love of Your Life* contend that there is a reliable, sanctioned route to follow. But they argue among themselves as to which one is best. So what is the single traveler to do?

I have a suggestion. Before you set out on your journey, get your bearings. In my research, I have had the opportunity to track the evolution of courtship in America. And that orientation has helped me to see how to proceed from this point forward. I think it might help you too. For one thing, you might be comforted to learn that this isn't the first time that single people have been confused about how to find a mate.

Some More History[4]

As one might suspect, the history of courtship runs parallel to the history of marriage narrated in chapter 6. As we noted, the biggest shift in patterns of mate selection began in Western countries during the 1700s when, over time, the arranged marriage was replaced by individual freedom to choose or refuse a partner. In colonial and post-revolution America, most courtship consisted of the social interactions that were integrated into everyday life. Young people chose marital partners over the span of a decade as they grew up together.

"Calling" (Women in Control)

In the nineteenth century, gender roles began to change. Men and women moved into separate spheres as the husband became *the* breadwinner and the wife's domain was the home. Courtship became more formalized.[5] Most courting was conducted in the girl's home under the watchful eyes (and ears) of parents.[6] The process was referred to as "calling," and the participants followed detailed rules of etiquette. Each step in the courtship was completely controlled by the young woman who instigated the visits by issuing an invitation (initially through her mother) to a prospective caller. And most of the courtship was conducted on her turf. The end goal of this system of courtship was understood by everyone involved: marriage.

"Dating" (Men in Control)

These elaborate customs of calling were limited to those upper- and middle-class families affluent enough to own a home with a parlor or front porch where the visits were conducted.[7] Working-class youth became innovative and courted in public. So instead of the man coming in, the woman went out with him to a restaurant, soda fountain, movie, or baseball game.[8] Over time, "dating" (as it was called) came to be widely practiced in all levels of society.

In *Wing to Wing, Oar to Oar*, historian Beth Bailey notes that "there was some confusion caused by this reversal of initiative, especially during the twenty years or so when going out and calling co-existed as systems."[9] By 1920, public dating had essentially supplanted private calling as the universal approach to courtship.

The shift from calling to dating changed more than where it was done. It brought about a major realignment in the balance of power at two levels. One change was generational: the dating system lessened parental control and gave greater autonomy to the dating couple. But the more striking change was the reversal of roles between men and women. When courtship took place in the home, the woman was the hostess who entertained her guest. But the invitation to go out was an invitation into the man's world, not only because a date took place in the public sphere (man's territory) but because he was paying for it.[10]

So he now took the initiative and exercised the prerogatives of a host. The advent of the automobile reinforced, accelerated, and expanded these trends.

As the culture of dating evolved between the two World Wars, dating came to be seen as distinct from courting. That is, dating became a vehicle for getting to know someone *before* pairing off with them in an exclusive relationship. The transition to courtship was made when a couple began keeping "steady company." This system of dating, going steady, getting engaged, and getting married is the paradigm that governed the romantic progressions of young adults through the 1950s and beyond. This was the "culturally set out" pathway to marriage referred to by professors Amy and Leon Kass.

"Hanging Out" and "Hooking Up" (No One in Control)

In the last third of the twentieth century, dramatic upheavals occurred in society that profoundly challenged the once-conventional views of human mating. One product of this social revolution is an alternative mating system that came into being alongside the established dating and courtship system that prevailed during the first two-thirds of the twentieth century. Social historian Barbara Dafoe Whitehead calls it a "Relationships System," and summarizes it in this way:

> It is not a romantic courtship and marriage system...The purposes of this emerging mating system are more diverse: it is designed for a variety of intimate pair-bonded arrangements, from marriage to living together to serial monogamy to sexual partnerings without any strings attached. This emerging mating system has no comprehensive "national" set of standards for romantic courtship. Nor is it likely that it ever will, given its diversity.[11]

So now the ways that men and women get together socially have greatly diversified. Alongside the more structured systems of dating are less formal approaches to connecting. Many singles are more inclined to hang out in groups at parties, clubs, and other social settings.

Individuals within the group may find a partner to "hook up" with—an ambiguous term that describes a one-time encounter that often includes sex. Whereas dating may initiate a relationship that progresses in the expression of romantic intimacy over time, hooking up typically features overt sexual interaction and goes nowhere relationally.[12]

Christian Alternatives

Many Christians have rightly reacted to the rise of the Relationships System with alarm. Its goals, values, motivations, behaviors, and consequences stand in opposition to a biblical worldview. Any believer whose schooling or employment places them in that cultural environment will have to battle those influences.

But even before these illicit encounters gained social acceptability, perceptive Christians began recognizing problems with traditional dating models widely practiced by believers. Some writers denounced the artificiality of dating experiences that produced romantic bonding within superficial relationships.[13] Others protested the impropriety of "recreational" romances characterized by erotic behaviors that ought to be reserved for the person one ultimately marries.[14]

The deficiencies of the dating system *as practiced by Christians* prompted Joshua Harris to write *I Kissed Dating Goodbye* (published in 1997).[15] His critique of the dating system and efforts to identify a more biblical approach to courtship resonated with a huge number of Christian singles. In some quarters, agreement with Harris's conclusions was so pervasive that the practice of dating was virtually shut down. Some went so far as to vilify dating as unbiblical, even sinful.

Courtship

Harris proposed replacing the culture of dating with a system of date-less courtship. It is distinguished from dating by its purpose: courtship is a process in which a man and woman of marriageable age intentionally explore the possibility of marriage. They do this by spending time together in a variety of settings, sharing in diverse experiences. Practitioners of courtship do not engage in casual or recreational dating. They reserve any interactions that might lead to romance for one person who is a likely candidate for matrimony. While some of their activities might look like dates, they make a point to guard their hearts, avoiding the pitfall of falling in love too soon. They are conscious of moving through phases in the development of their relationship—from casual friendship, to deeper friendship, to purposeful intimacy with integrity, to engagement.[16] The courtship process may be terminated by either party at any juncture prior to a wedding.

In *5 Paths to the Love of Your Life,* Douglas Wilson describes a variation of the courtship approach that adds one dimension—"the active, involved authority of the young woman's father (or head of the household) in the formation of her romantic attachments leading to marriage."[17] In this arrangement, any man interested in cultivating a personal relationship with a woman must gain the approval of her father. As the protector of his daughter's best interests, the father's blessing must be secured before an engagement can be declared.

Betrothal

In the father-approved version of courtship, the pendulum swings back in the direction of the arranged marriage. But for some, it doesn't swing far enough. And so a third system, called betrothal, has also been proposed. In this paradigm, the distinctive feature added to the mix is *front-end commitment.* If a man identifies a woman that he finds suitable or desirable as a wife, he approaches her father and expresses his interest. If the parents and the woman give their consent, the man and woman become betrothed—that is, decisively engaged to be married. It is understood by all involved that the betrothal is binding; this couple *will* marry at the agreed upon time. It is only after this commitment is made that the couple enter into the process that, in the other systems, constitutes courtship. The period of betrothal is a time of preparation authorizing the couple to begin "releasing their hearts to one another."[18]

Dating Reconsidered

One other reaction to Joshua Harris's declaration of war against dating moved in a different direction. When counselors Henry Cloud and John Townsend read Harris's book, they identified with the pain and disillusionment experienced by so many singles who had been wounded through dating. But while they validated the reasons behind the no-dating movement, they disagreed with the proposed solution. "This is a little like saying because there is divorce, no one should get married."[19] It isn't necessary to throw the baby out with the bath water, they argued. What Christian singles need to kiss goodbye is *defective* dating.

Taking Responsibility

Having surveyed the options, we now return to the question of which map you should use. It is a question with two parts. First we must ask: *Is there a biblically prescribed method for mate selection?*

The short answer is no.[20] It is true that there is one dominant approach throughout biblical history—the arranged marriage.[21] It is also true that the Mosaic Law regulated some behaviors connected with acquiring a spouse. But we do not find directives that require a believer to follow a specific approach in mate selection. (In making this point, Ben Young and Samuel Adams provide a humorous list of "Top Ten 'Biblical Ways' to Find a Mate," starting with: "10. Find a prostitute and marry her [Hos. 1:1-3]."[22])

The Bible provides an explanation of what constitutes marriage. But it prescribes no system for *choosing* the person one marries. Rather than telling us what process to follow, the prophets and apostles gave instructions on how God's people should act as they applied the societal norms of the cultures they lived in.[23]

In the absence, then, of specific instructions on mate selection, these deliberations are "non-commanded decisions," which entail freedom and responsibility on the part of the individual. Whatever approach you take must comply with God's moral will and with wisdom.

"So if there is no biblically prescribed method for mate selection, what should I do?" you ask. R. Paul Stevens provides the answer: "In reality there are only two ways to get married: have an arranged marriage (someone else does the arranging) or arrange one yourself!"[24] You must take the responsibility to develop a wisdom-shaped plan to guide your search for a mate. (I will try to help you. That's why there's one more chapter in this book.)

Imagining Courtship

Before you identify the specific elements of your plan, you need to determine the courting model you intend to follow. But rather than choose between a dating model, a courtship model, or a betrothal model,[25] I believe it is preferable to use key elements of all three approaches.

In their book *Soul Virgins,* Doug Rosenau and Michael Todd Wilson provide a helpful image of crossing a bridge. In their scenario, the mating journey involves movement through three stages: connecting, coupling, and covenanting.[26]

The Relationship Continuum Bridge

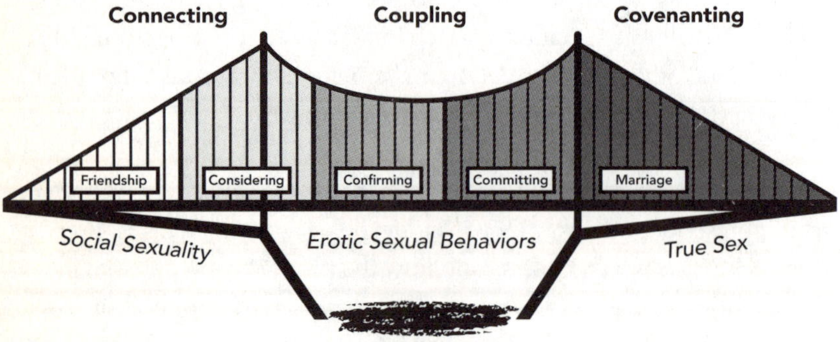

The journey begins with the development of *connecting* relationships, which include friendships and casual dating. The focus is on building skills for interactions with opposite-sex friends. At the other end of the continuum is *covenanting* or marriage. This is where an exclusive relationship with a single mate is formalized and lived out in one-flesh union. Bridging the beginning and ending stages is the intermediate *coupling* phase where a man and woman interact as an exclusive (yet unmarried) couple.

The coupling stage, where the courting pair actually "crosses the bridge," entails moving through three subphases: considering, confirming, and committing.

Considering: This stage begins when the woman and man agree to date exclusively. Now the process of evaluating the other as a potential life partner begins in earnest.

Confirming: This is sometimes described as the stage when the couple is "engaged to be engaged." During this period, the couple explores any and all issues that may affect a future marriage. This is most effectively accomplished through pre-engagement counseling.

Committing: This is formal engagement. The intention to marry is publicly announced and plans are set in motion for a wedding.

The Role of Dating

The adoption of this framework for courting presumes that it is not necessary to completely reject the notion of dating. I agree with Cloud and Townsend that there is such a thing as healthy dating that most couples can employ as they approach and cross the bridge.

In my advocacy of dating, I'm assuming an encounter that is not sinful by definition. I think we will be on safe ground if we start with a broad definition extracted from the dictionary: "a prearranged social engagement; a time set aside beforehand, social in nature."[27] In our culture, some purposeful, social, personal interaction appears to be required in order for a man and woman to explore and cultivate the kind of relationship that could develop into a courtship.

In evaluating the relative merits and liabilities of dating, we start with the moral will of God. Does the Bible command dating? No. Does the Bible forbid dating? No. Does the Bible say anything about dating? Not directly. There were no social categories in biblical culture that correspond precisely to the contemporary practice of dating. So once again we are talking about issues that lie within the area of freedom and responsibility.

However, that does not mean that the moral will of God has no bearing at all on dating. For Scripture has a lot to say about how men and women ought to relate to each other. This includes the Great Commandment,[28] all of the "one another" passages,[29] as well as the texts that address moral concerns.[30] So while dating is a neutral activity as far as the Bible is concerned, those who practice it should do so wisely and Christianly.

The apostle Paul told the Corinthians that one way to evaluate the appropriateness of a morally neutral activity is to ask: "Is it beneficial? Is it constructive?" (1 Corinthians 6:12; 10:23). It is precisely in those terms that Cloud and Townsend make their case for healthy dating:

1. Dating gives people the opportunity to learn about themselves, others, and relationships in a safe context.
2. Dating provides a context to work through issues.
3. Dating helps build relationship skills.
4. Dating can heal and repair. (A date is not the proper venue for therapy, but a positive dating experience is good for the soul.)
5. Dating is relational and has value in and of itself.
6. Dating lets someone learn what he or she likes in the opposite sex.
7. Dating gives a context to learn sexual self-control and other delay of gratification.[31]

Dating in isolation from other forms of social interaction will not provide sufficient experience to get to know another person in depth. But constructive and enjoyable dates can contribute a lot to the participants as well as to their relationship. As a couple proceeds to cross the bridge, their experience of dating will reflect their growing relationship and provide a context for increasing intimacy with integrity.

• • • • • • • •

With your profile of a keeper in hand and a functional framework for courtship in place, you are now in a position to consider the specific elements in your plan to look for a mate.

Don't Forget...

- While the journey from singleness to marriage is challenging, Christians can be thankful for God-given resources their secular peers lack.
- Since there is no biblically prescribed method for mate selection, you must take the responsibility to develop your own wisdom-shaped plan to guide your search for a mate.
- "The Relationship Continuum Bridge" provides a coherent description of the progressive phases of courtship: connecting, coupling (considering, confirming, committing), and covenanting.
- Most couples who eventually marry will have engaged in some form of dating en route. Healthy dating will be beneficial to the process if done wisely and righteously.

To access the endnotes and for questions for reflection and group discussion go to:

www.TheMarriageDecision.com

CHAPTER 15

Courtship: Devising the Plan

Amusement parks around the country offer many exciting attractions. Some rides, however, are too thrilling for small children. Little ones are denied access for their own safety. The barrier to admission is usually a sign that says, "You must be this tall to enter this attraction." Sometimes a cartoon character cutout with its arm extended indicates the minimum height. And children are required to measure themselves to see if they are big enough to go on the ride.

Are You Big Enough?

The courtship bridge is for adults. But not everybody who is old enough is also mature and healthy enough to venture across it. For before you begin to seriously look for a mate, you need to be ready for marriage. So for your own safety, you need to pause and take your own measure before proceeding.

The person who is prepared to actively look for a mate should meet the following conditions:

- You are a grown-up-and-growing adult.
- You are emotionally healthy.
- You have a life (you don't *need* to get married to be OK).
- You understand God's design for marriage and are committed to it.
- You know yourself well.

- You have established boundaries of moral behavior.
- You have constructed your profile of a keeper.
- You are pursuing godly character.
- You have good friends.

If any of these characteristics are not in place, you may need to focus your energies on self-preparation rather than looking for Mr. or Ms. Right.

Taking Responsibility

One reason you need to be big enough for the bridge is that you will likely have to take some initiative to move across it. The vehicles of courtship that folks formerly used to get from one side to the other are considered outmoded in many quarters. Maybe that's not the case where you live. But if the mechanisms of courtship in your area are in disrepair or broken down, you may have to reinvent the wheel.

That's not all bad. One advantage of living in a time and culture where the dating systems are in flux is that men and women can create a plan that will work for them. In a context of freedom, there's plenty of room for creativity. What's required is the willingness to take personal responsibility for developing, implementing, and communicating the plan to whomever else may be involved.

Christian women have to decide how much initiative they are willing to take in starting a relationship with a man. In my view, there are two ways to think about this.

On the one hand, plenty of precedent exists for women to set courtship in motion. One biblical illustration is Ruth. Following the counsel of her mother-in-law, Naomi, Ruth took some dramatic steps to establish a special relationship with Boaz. In fact, she is the one who proposed marriage. And the whole system of "calling" in vogue at the turn of the twentieth century gave control of the proceedings to women. So you don't have to sit back and wait for a man to act.

You may be hoping for a man who will show his willingness to lead in a relationship by taking the initiative. And you may meet one. But men do not tend to be as relationally oriented as women. Louise saw the potential for our match long before I did. Sometimes you have to emulate the farmer who whacked his inert mule between the eyes with a two-by-four and said, "First, you have to get his attention." When Ruth "got his attention," Boaz stepped up and provided leadership from that point forward.[1] I did the same.

But if you are reluctant to be seen as too aggressive, you are hardly without recourse in influencing a man in the direction he ought to go. Many men would eagerly respond to signals of interest from enterprising women. But if subtle isn't working, you could always walk up to the guy and say, "If you ask me out for coffee, I would be glad to go."

And now a word to the men: Read the previous four paragraphs and figure it out! Just do it.

Do What?

"In reality there are only two ways to get married: have an arranged marriage (someone else does the arranging) or arrange one yourself!"[2] For single people who live in Western culture, this summary of options by R. Paul Stevens presents not two realistic choices but one. If you get married, you're probably going to have to arrange it yourself.

But what does that mean exactly? This is a good place to remember the wise counsel of Larry Crabb: "Pray for your desires; work for your goals."[3] Your *desire*, in this case, is marriage. But since that involves the cooperation of another person, you cannot accomplish this by yourself. So pray about it. (This, by the way, is more important than everything that follows.)

What would be a legitimate *goal* that could potentially contribute to achieving what you desire? Here's my suggestion: work to *put yourself in position* to begin and cultivate relationships—one of which might culminate in marriage. That's what Louise did. Every time I turned around, there she was. She kept finding creative ways to be in the neighborhood until I noticed her. She also found ways to let me know of her interest without coming on too strong.

So if the overall objective is to position yourself for relationship, what does that involve? It will probably require several intermediate steps of two kinds: *tasks* to accomplish ("What do I need to do?") and *means* to carry them out ("*How* am I going to do that?"). The steps you come up with will constitute your plan.

I have identified some tasks that I think everyone needs to accomplish to get to the desired destination. Here are some suggestions to get you started.

The Tasks of Courtship

Task 1: You need ways to meet prospective mates.

If you attend a large church or are a student in a Christian college, this may not be a huge problem for you. You may have an adequate pool of prospects available. This can be more challenging for that large segment of single adults who are out of school and pursuing a career or other life interests. Whatever the reasons, if your pool of contacts is too limited, you will have to do something to expand it.

Henry Cloud offers this profound grasp of the obvious: *"People who meet people go where people are"* (italics his). Then, to be practical, he offers this list of places where singles have met their future spouse:[4]

1. Visit churches.
2. Talk to your friends (close and extended) about setting you up. (By the way, this is the most common means by which single people meet future spouses.)
3. Attend events sponsored by organizations.
4. Go to parties or plan some of your own.
5. Join organizations and activities related to your interests.
6. Check the newspaper and Web. Most papers have local activities postings.
7. Start something up. As an example, Cloud tells of a group of women who hosted a monthly event called SWARM (Single Women Actively Recruiting Men).
8. Seek out and attend cultural events.

9. Visit single vacation and recreational spots.
10. Exercise at the place where they are.
11. Take a class.
12. Join your coworkers when they go out.

My niece is one of the many Christian singles who have found the person they eventually married through an online dating or matching service. This doesn't work for everyone, but there is no reason not to investigate the possibilities that this modern-day phenomenon might open up. The first rule to practice in your exploration is safety. Find out the precautions the service has established and go through the proper channels. Be cautious about giving out personal information, and conduct the first meetings in public places. The second rule is to be persistent. Most people don't find their keeper on the first match. It may take quantity to get quality.[5]

Task 2: You need ways to acquire the social skills necessary for relationship building.

Most of the required social skills are naturally developed in routine interactions with people at school, work, and church. We become more or less adept at communicating and connecting with people as we form friendships. Dating requires different nuances, however, that are best learned in the specific experience of dating. This may be the best reason for casual dating—just learning how to do it. If you actually were to cross paths with Mr. or Ms. Right, but you lacked the skills to express yourself and actively engage with their self-disclosures, you could miss the opportunity that was presented. So the message here is practice, practice, practice.

Dating coach Henry Cloud offers sage advice to singles who are entry-level daters (at the front end of the "connecting" stage). One of his maxims is, "Dating is not about marriage." Those who submit to his tutelage must take the following pledge:

> I will date as an end in and of itself. I will no longer see dating as a place only to find a mate, but as a place to learn,

grow, experience, and serve other people. It is my new laboratory of learning, growth, and experience.

The corollary to his understanding of dating is this follow-up advice: Go out with almost anyone once, and maybe again. At the beginning, the requirements you have for a *date* should not be as stringent as the specifications you have established for a *mate*. The main reason is simple: you can't know whether a date has a potential mate's qualities until you get to know them. So on your first date(s), leave the profile at home. Just have fun![6]

This is one area where coaching, whether written, video, or personal, can be helpful. Cloud's book *How to Get a Date Worth Keeping* is remarkably practical and comprehensive.[7] Much of the content in that book is also available in brief video clips on the website of Drs. Cloud and Townsend at www.cloudtownsend.com.

For personal advice, you will need to recruit one or more mentors. Talking with experienced friends who will candidly share their insights could help you identify blind spots. Perhaps the best approach would be to find a friend who would be willing to read through Dr. Cloud's book with you and help you develop strategies for expanding your social skills and experiences.

Task 3: You need ways to get to know another person very well.

John Van Epp coined the term *know-quo* (the quotient for knowing someone) to describe this task. He helpfully summarizes the component parts in a mathematical formula: I = T + T + T. **I**ntimacy equals **T**alk (mutual self-disclosure) plus **T**ogetherness (diversified experiences) plus **T**ime. "A balance is necessary between what you know about a person from talking and what you learn from your experiences in a new relationship…Therefore, to truly know another person, you must engage in a deepening openness that is matched with a variety of experiences in which you see the other person 'in action.' "[8]

Maxson's Maxims

After surveying what is going on in the dating world, I have a couple of suggestions of my own. First, practice two categories of dating: *social* dates and *service* dates. These categories correspond to the two functions of marriage: relational companionship and working partnership.

Social dating is the dominant form in our culture. Typical dates seek shared experiences of entertainment or recreation that offer the opportunity to advance the relationship. These kinds of dates are appropriate and necessary for extended conversation. If the chemistry is positive, romance may ensue. But this sort of interaction is insufficient to produce an adequate level of *know-quo* required for marriage.

Shared involvement in *service* offers opportunities to get to know the other person in different and important ways. Before we began going out, Louise and I worked together on a worship team. Then we were fellow staff members for a junior high snow retreat. In a variety of ways, we were able to observe each other and participate together in work and ministry situations. (The same was true, you may recall, for Ruth and Boaz.) If you are interested in someone, suggest joint participation in a service or ministry project. Work together with a youth group, help out in the church nursery, volunteer for a community-service event, go on a short-term mission trip.

I recommend that you give a priority to service dates over social dates for three reasons. First, you may find that an invitation to share in a ministry project is less threatening and easier to accept. Second, service dates provide a better setting for demonstrating and evaluating the more significant components of your profile—character and commitment (but also comparability and complementarity). And third, starting out with service-related interactions follows the sequence in the arranged marriage where a couple launches the work partnership first and grows the relational companionship over time.

But whether a given date is social or service-oriented, approach it (and your date) with a *ministry mindset.* If I could paraphrase Jesus and his Sermon on the Mount: "You shall not be like the pagans who go on dates mainly to impress the other person and evaluate their suitability to meet your needs. Instead, seek to advance God's rule and righteousness in the life of your date, and these other things will be properly ordered in your relationship." Think of your date as a brother or sister in Christ and treat them accordingly, applying the "one another" commands to your relationship. Should you someday marry, you will be well practiced in one of the central purposes of your union. Also, you will probably be more relaxed and have more fun.

Court the Family

Whether you choose to follow Maxson's Maxims or not, you must find ways to enter into the other person's world—work, family, friends, recreation, service, and worship—in order to truly know (and be known by) them. You will learn a great deal about a person when you observe their interactions with their parents and siblings, as well as their friends. You need to see if you integrate comfortably into that world (and they into yours), because if you get married, those people will become part of your life. Furthermore, the way your prospect interacts with family members (especially the parent and siblings of the opposite gender) will give you a good picture of how you can expect them to relate to you in your marriage. And their choice of friends will reveal a lot about their character.

In other words, you don't just court the individual; you must also court that person's family and friends.

If it looks like the relationship has the potential to culminate in marriage, *pre-engagement counseling* will help to surface any background, emotional, or relational issues that need to be addressed. It should also provide a format for identifying relational skills that need to be learned as well as a guided opportunity to practice and grow in those abilities.

Task 4: You need to learn how to balance and manage agapé, philos, and eros.

When a couple comes to me for premarital counseling and I ask why they want to get married, their first answer is often, "Because we love each other." From a biblical perspective, that's not a bad place to start. For the New Testament is clear that husbands are to love their wives, and wives are to love their husbands (Ephesians 5:25,33; Titus 2:4).

But as the ancient Greeks perceptively discerned, love is multidimensional. So they had a distinctive word for each nuance. *Eros* is the kind of love expressed by *erotic passion.*[9] *Philos* most closely corresponds to the mutual affection expressed and enjoyed in friendship.[10] The apostles co-opted the word *agapé* to describe sacrificial, self-giving love that is bestowed with no thought of a return from the other.[11]

It may be overly simplistic to say that in a marriage *agapé* fuels the partnership, *philos* warms the companionship, and *eros* drives the lovemaking that results in procreation. But it is clear that a good marriage is enhanced by all three shades of love as they become interwoven in the fabric of life. One of the tasks of courtship is to cultivate the integration of all three aspects of love in a way that strengthens the relationship and prepares for marriage.

You need to grow *agapé,* deepen *philos,* and manage *eros.*

As we have seen, kingdom marriage recognizes the priority of *agapé.* Such Christlike love protects the beloved from the abuses of unfettered *eros* during courtship and superintends its expression during marriage. A*gapé* guards the heart and allows *philos* to grow into a devoted companionship that will enrich a marriage for a lifetime. (A*gapé* is the missing ingredient in cohabitation.)

And so, even as a dating couple grows in the deepening of their friendship and delights in the measured enjoyment of burgeoning romance, each must give attention to cultivating *agapé* that will sustain the commitment of the covenant. This quality of selflessness cannot be produced by sheer determination or effort. It is a fruit of the Spirit. And so the highest form of devotion that one person can show another is to pursue the higher love that enables such devotion. *Your growing relationship with God is the most important aspect of a courtship that issues in a godly and fulfilling marriage.*

Managing Eros

I have already pounded the pulpit on the intoxicating effects of twitterpation. "Choose your spouse with your heart, not your head" was number one on my hit parade of ways to torpedo a marriage. In my warnings I do not intend to disparage romance. Lauren Winner restores an appreciative perspective by pointing out that "the exhilarating experience we call falling in love, can actually teach us something about loving our neighbor." Then she cites theologian Diogenes Allen:

> When falling in love, we seem to float on air. The whole world seems wonderful, and we take in stride people who normally irritate us and the things that normally frustrate us...For a while, we simply seem to be able to love anyone—to love our neighbor—without any effort at all. These momentary occasions can...give us a glimpse of what it would be like to love our neighbor all the time.[12]

But *eros* finds its consummating expression in sexual intercourse. Romantic passion continually builds toward a crescendo intended to climax on a couple's wedding night—and beyond. But not before. And so while romance is not something to be avoided by mature Christians, it must be managed. Though Cupid's euphoria is very powerful, it does not completely incapacitate your mind and will. *Agapé* must exercise the discipline to establish protective limits on the expression of *eros* during courtship. One of the best ways to maintain a semblance of sanity while under the influence is to think through a management plan before the arrow strikes.

For instance, a good idea to set and communicate boundaries toward the beginning of the relationship as to how affection will be expressed and phased in over the course of the courtship. This kind of decision making shows respect for the other person and will give both of you a sense of security as the relationship progresses.[13]

Another step is to call in the cavalry. One of the biggest flaws in the romance-based dating system is that relationships are carried out in isolation from an engaged community. (Community involvement was one of the strengths of the arranged marriage format.) Even though marital decisions lie in the area of freedom and responsibility, wisdom directs you to consult with counselors. So recruit a team of people you can trust to oversee your courtship—accountability partners, a small group, mentors, wise friends. Henry Cloud writes, "The only rule is that you must make yourself vulnerable to them, submit to them, put it all out there for them to see, and consider the wisdom, feedback, challenges, and correction they offer you."[14]

As you consult counselors, do not overlook the potential benefit of giving your parents a prominent role as members of that team, if possible. In previous eras, ancient and enduring wisdom gave the assignment of mate selection to them. Even if the systems of parent-directed courtship and betrothal are not biblically mandated, one should not ignore the sensibleness of paying heed to the counsel of those who know us best and truly have our best interests at heart.

Task 5: You need to get your "person of interest" on board with your approach so that you are traveling together.

One way to do this would be to ask them to read a copy of this book and then discuss how the principles and insights are going to shape the conduct of your relationship.

And if you become engaged, arrange for premarital counseling from someone who can offer practical, biblical guidance.

Five Tasks of a Highly Effective Plan

Task 1: You need ways to meet prospective mates.

Task 2: You need ways to acquire the social skills necessary for relationship building.

Task 3: You need ways to get to know another person very well.

Task 4: You need to learn how to balance and manage *agapé, philos,* and *eros.*

Task 5: You need to get your "person of interest" on board with your approach so that you are traveling together.

Don't Forget...

- Crossing the courtship bridge is restricted to healthy grown-ups. Before you begin to seriously look for a mate, you need to be ready for marriage.

- As you construct a plan to find a mate, your objective is to *put yourself in position* to begin and cultivate relationships—one of which might culminate in marriage.
- As you work your plan, pray for your desires.

....

RECOMMENDED READING

How to Get a Date Worth Keeping by Dr. Henry Cloud (Zondervan).

....

To access the endnotes and for questions for reflection and group discussion go to:

www.TheMarriageDecision.com

EPILOGUE

And They Lived Happily Ever After

Did you notice that I never finished the Story of Marriage?

I got as far as Act 3, "Jesus Remade It." Then we stopped to work on your plan for looking for a mate. That was appropriate because the third act is the one we happen to live in. During this age, God is acting in Christ to restore what was ruined, to reconcile what was alienated, and to recover what was lost. And he has invited us to participate in that project by advancing his rule and righteousness within our own lives and throughout our world. Our marital status, whether we are single or married, is the platform from which we carry out this mission. Act 3 is still in progress.

But how will it end? And does it matter?

In the romantic fairy tales, the climax of the story is the rescue of the fair maiden by the gallant knight. They marry and live happily ever after. The wedding is the end of the story. (Apparently, whatever happens after that is not interesting enough to tell about.)

As we come to the end of this book, we have left some stories hanging. Whatever became of Julie and Jay and Nancy? Did they find the spouses they were hoping for? The outcomes of their quests remain unwritten.

And then there's *your* story—the one you care about. Will you find a mate? I don't know.

What I do know is this: if you find a spouse and get married, that will not be the end of the story. That's because your marital adventure is a subplot in a cosmic romance, and it isn't finished yet.

But we know how it will turn out.

"'Til Death Do Us Part"

Act 4 in the Story of Marriage concerns the age to come—when Christ reigns over a redeemed community of people inhabiting a renewed, perfected earth, dwelling in eternal fellowship with and service to him (Revelation 21–22).

In the Bible, we don't find a lot of verses devoted to Act 4. And what they say about marriage is paradoxical. One sentence informs us that *none* of us will be married in heaven. Other passages are very clear that *all* believers in Jesus will be married.

The first part comes from Jesus himself in a single statement: "For in the resurrection [people] neither marry nor are given in marriage, but are like angels in heaven" (Matthew 22:30).

Just as his instruction on marriage in the present age was prompted by conniving Pharisees, this time his baiters were Sadducees, a different religious party. Disbelieving in the resurrection, these academic posers sought to demonstrate the absurdity of resurrection by creating a hypothetical scenario in which one woman (through the law of levirate marriage—Deuteronomy 25:5-10) could end up married to seven brothers.[1] "In the resurrection," they smirked, "whose wife of the seven will she be?" (Matthew 22:28).

Like a veteran astronaut explaining to children that the moon is not made of cheese, Jesus gave them enough information to demonstrate that they were out of their league. And from that exchange we learn what we would not otherwise know—that human marriage belongs to earthly life only.[2]

When a bride and groom set the temporal limits on their marital commitment with the words, "'til death do us part," they are speaking the truth. Death terminates the covenant (Romans 7:2). In heaven, no one will be married to the person (or persons) they were wed to on earth. We will all be single.[3]

I don't know how the Sadducees reacted to this information, but I have to admit that the first time I heard it, I was disappointed. As a happily married man who really enjoys his wife, I didn't relish the prospect of that relationship coming to an end. And it seemed inappropriate to be reacting to information about heaven with a feeling of loss.

I subsequently learned a couple of things that changed my perspective. The first is that my love for my wife and hers for me will in no way be diminished. Quite the opposite—our love will be set free from the limitations of living in a fallen world. Michael J. Wilkins explains:

> While the state of relationships will be altered at the resurrection, this does not imply that prior earthly relationships are eliminated completely, nor does it imply that resurrected relationships are without special attachment. The wife (or husband, for that matter) of multiple spouses in this life will have an equally altered capacity and understanding of love, which will enable her (or him) to love all without measure or jealousy or possessiveness.[4]

Is that cool or what?

We Will All Experience It

The second mitigating factor is the other half of the paradox: all of us collectively will be married—to King Jesus. For the wedding anticipated by the apostle Paul in Ephesians 5:25-27 and 2 Corinthians 11:2 has already been witnessed in the futuristic vision of the apostle John in Revelation 19:7-8; 21:2,9-14. As Ray Ortlund Jr. says, "There will be no human marriages in heaven...for heaven will be *the* marriage."[5]

> The people of God will be 'like angels in heaven,' in that the centre of their existence will be undivided communion with God. Then the beautiful and delicate interplay of man and woman with one another will give way to the ultimate reality of Christ and his church for ever at one.[6]

When Louise and I stand together in the presence of Jesus in the company of the saints, I don't expect to be thinking, "Gee, it's too bad we're not married to each other anymore." If we think about our earthly marriage at all, we might say to ourselves, "So *this* is what that was about."

Perhaps you will recall that part of God's design for marriage is that it be a reflection of the union between Christ and his church.[7] Human marriage was always intended to point beyond itself to something ultimate. In our earthly experience, marriage is the concrete thing, the known from which we gain insight into the unknown. But when we arrive in heaven, we will encounter the real thing. Then we will learn that we have been living all along in marital "shadowlands."[8] We will see that human marriage, at its very best, was giving us only the slightest glimpse of the glory that is to come in the "true marriage." And when that happens, we will not be reluctant to lay aside earthly marriage "the way a picture is no longer needed when you see face to face."[9]

This is why I titled Act 4: "We Will All Experience It." All believers in Jesus will enter into the ultimate marital union with him, of which the best human marriages are but a shadow.

So What?

I see two major benefits of knowing how The Story culminates. The first is the reminder that human marriage is not the ultimate relationship. Sometimes, as we exercise our stewardship during Act 3, we need help keeping marriage in its place. Recognizing that earthly marriage is optional, secondary, pictorial, and temporary can help us maintain the priority of our allegiance to the lordship of Jesus Christ.

The second value for single Christians comes from knowing and believing this promise: *Even if you never experience human marriage in this life, you will not be denied the fullest blessings of marriage in the age to come.*[10] In the glorified community of the redeemed, every one of us will be single, and all relational restrictions that separated the married from the unmarried on a fallen planet will be removed. And all of us, together, will be married to King Jesus. I do not know how much of our former marital status we will remember; but I am confident that we will feel no more loss than a butterfly feels having shed its cocoon.

And because this is no fairy tale, the wedding of the King and his Bride will not be the end of the story. You have reached the conclusion of this book. But I'm going to borrow the closing words from *The Chronicles of Narnia* by C.S. Lewis to remind us how Act 4 plays out:

> The things that began to happen after that were so great and beautiful that I cannot write them...But for them it

> was only the beginning of the real story. All their life in this world and all their adventures in Narnia had only been the cover and the title page: now at last they were beginning Chapter One of the Great Story which no one on earth has read: which goes on forever: in which every chapter is better than the one before.[11]

Don't Forget...

- In the age to come, all believers in Jesus will be single and all relational restrictions that separated the married from the unmarried on a fallen planet will be removed.
- In the age to come, all believers in Jesus will be married—to King Jesus. That is when we will experience the fulfillment of the most wonderful aspects of love foreshadowed in human marriage.
- One reason single Christians can make sacrificial choices about marriage in this life is that they have the promise of the fullest experience of marriage in the age to come.

To access the endnotes and for questions for reflection and group discussion go to:

www.TheMarriageDecision.com

Singleness, Marriage, and the Will of God

Not everyone will marry or should, but virtually all single adults think about marriage. And all make decisions that either maintain their singleness or attempt to change it.

This book, by the authors of the groundbreaking *Decision Making and the Will of God*, offers an in-depth tutorial to help singles apply biblical principles to the critical choices they confront:

- Do I want to get married? Are there good reasons to remain single?
- What sort of person should I consider as a potential spouse?
- How do I look for a mate?
- What should I do if no spouse shows up?
- What is God's role in the decision-making process?

This comprehensive volume will equip readers to make wise choices about marriage according to the will of God. It's also an invaluable resource for parents, counselors, and pastors.